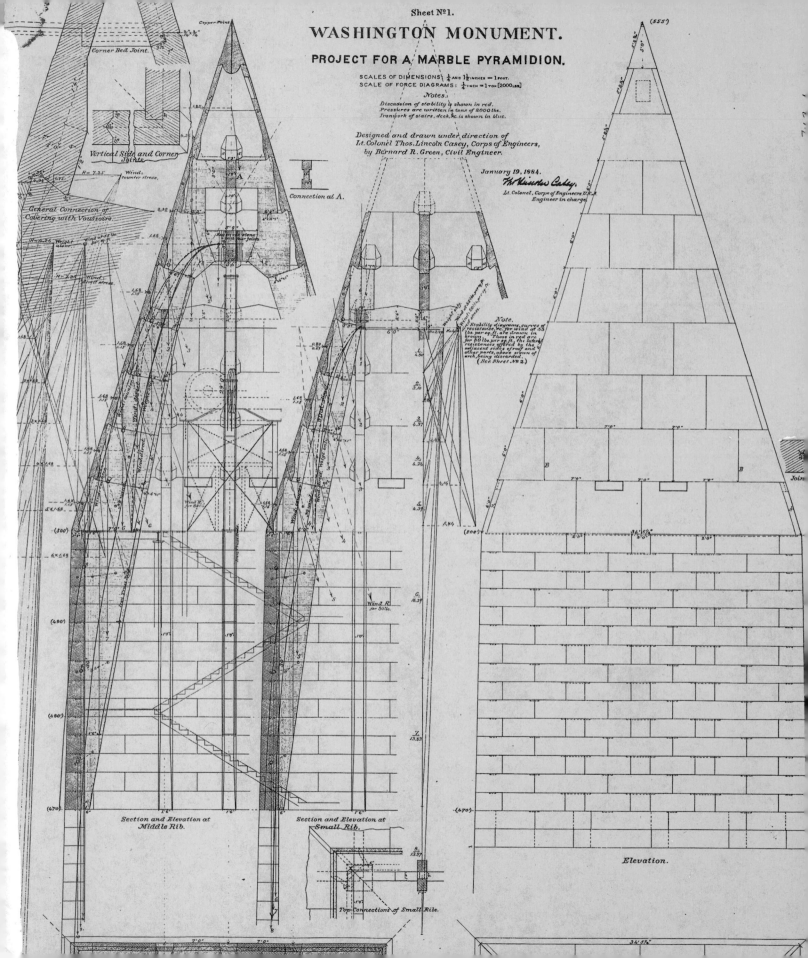

1995: THE MILLION MAN MARCH

THE WASHINGTON MONUMENT

IT STANDS FOR ALL

THOMAS B. ALLEN

DISCOVERY BOOKS

PREVIOUS PAGES

page 1: Detailed plans for the Monument's pyramidion, 1884.

pages 2-3: The Washington Monument on a night in the 1930s.

Discovery Communications, Inc.

John S. Hendricks   *Founder, Chairman, and Chief Executive Officer*
Judith A. McHale   *President and Chief Operating Officer*
Judy L. Harris   *Senior Vice President and General Manager,
Consumer Products*

Discovery Channel Publishing

Natalie Chapman   *Vice President, Publishing*
Rita Thievon Mullin   *Editorial Director*
Mary Kalamaras   *Senior Editor*
Maria Mihalik Higgins   *Editor*
Michael Hentges   *Design Director*
Rick Ludwick   *Managing Editor*
Heather Quinlan   *Editorial Coordinator*
Christine Alvarez   *Business Development*
Jill Gordon   *Marketing Manager*

Executive Editor, book and cover design

Bill Marr   *Open Books, LLC, Edgewater, Maryland*

Discovery Communications, Inc., produces high-quality television programming, interactive media, books, films, and consumer products. Discovery Networks, a division of Discovery Communications, Inc., operates and manages the Discovery Channel, TLC, Animal Planet, Travel Channel, and the Discovery Health Channel.

Discovery Communications website address: www.discovery.com
Random House website address: www.randomhouse.com

Printed in the United States on acid-free paper
10 9 8 7 6 5 4 3 2 1
First Edition

Library of Congress Cataloging-in-Publication Data
on file with the Library of Congress

ILLUSTRATION CREDITS

Library of Congress
pages: 7 (top, second from top, bottom), 13, 27, 29 (top, lower left), 30, 37, 39, 41, 42, 44-45, 47, 49, 50-51, 53, 55, 57 (top left, top right), 59, 63, 66-67, 72, 75 (both), 76-77, 78, 81, 96 (inset, upper right), 102, 103, 104 (both), 106-107, 108-109, 110, 111, 115, 120-121, 123, 124-125, 136, 140-141 (all), 148, 168-169 (top), 171.

National Archives
pages: 1, 7 (third from top), 16-17, 20, 23, 29 (lower right), 33, 35, 38, 54, 56, 57 (top middle, lower right), 60-61, 62, 64, 65, 69, 70 (left middle, left bottom), 73, 134-135.

District of Columbia Public Library
Washingtoniana Division and the Washington Star Collection; Copyright Washington Post; Reprinted by permission of the D. C. Public Library
pages: 133, 137, 138, 142, 143, 145, 172.

pp 2-3: ©Volkmar Wentzel; **p 4:** ©Pete Souza/Liaison Agency; **p 8:** ©Reuters/ Gary Cameron/Archive Photos; **p 10:** Mount Vernon Ladies Association; **p 11:** Open Books, LLC; **p 24:** National Portrait Gallery, Smithsonian Institution/ Art Resource, NY; **p 31:** (upper right, inset) USGS; **p 52:** F. C. Minor/ National Geographic Society Image Collection; **p 71:** Bill Marr/Open Books LLC; **pp 80-95:** all memorial stones, David Baratz/Discovery Channel Communications; **p 96:** (inset, second from top) Bill Marr/Open Books LLC; **p 97:** (inset, right) David Baratz/Discovery Channel Communications; **p 99:** ©Todd Eberle; **p 100:** (top) Bill Marr/Open Books LLC; **p 100:** (middle) John Spaulding/Discovery Channel Communications; **p 100:** (bottom) Dennis Brack/Discovery Channel Communications; **p 101:** Dennis Brack/Discovery Channel Communications; **p 105:** National Park Service; **pp 112-113:** Marrleen Collection; **p 117:** ©Corbis; **pp 118-119:** (both) Maynard Williams/National Geographic Society Image Collection; **p 120:** left, Maynard Williams/National Geographic Society Image Collection; **pp 126-127:** ©Volkmar Wentzel; **p 129:** ©Bettman/ CORBIS; **pp 130-131:** ©Bettman/CORBIS; **p 132:** ©Bettman/CORBIS; **p139:** ©Washington Post; **pp 146-147:** ©Flip Schulke/Black Star; **p 149:** ©Bettman/ CORBIS; **pp 150-151:** ©Robert Houston/Black Star; **p 153:** ©CORBIS; **pp 154-155:** ©Dennis Brack/ Black Star; **p 156:** ©Roland Freeman/Magnum; **p 157:** ©Dennis Brack/Black Star; **pp 158-159:** ©Richard Vogel/Liaison Agency; **p 160:** ©Lisa Quinones/Black Star; **p 161:** ©Lisa Quinones/Black Star; **pp 162-163:** ©Eli Reed/Magnum; **p 164:** ©Michael Williamson/Washington Post; **p 165:** ©Dennis Brack/Black Star; **p 167:** ©Wally McNamee/CORBIS; **pp168-169:** (bottom) Bill Marr/Open Books, LLC.

Washington Monument illustration, pp 96-98: ©Wm Pitzer, PitzoGraphics.

CONTENTS

By Stephen E. Ambrose

Our nation's capital abounds with statues to our heroes, led by the Lincoln Memorial, the Jefferson Memorial, and the FDR Memorial. Many of its finest buildings, the White House, the Capitol, and the Smithsonian Institution museums among them, have symbolic as well as working purposes.

The memorial that stands out, by far, is the Washington Monument. Besides being the tallest and the most immediately recognized, it is the grandest and the most superbly designed. It is our tribute to the man who led our nation to victory in the Revolutionary War and who, as our first President, did more than anyone else to create our Republic.

Thomas Jefferson extended the nation from the Mississippi River to the Rocky Mountains. Abraham Lincoln preserved it. Franklin Roosevelt led it to triumph in the greatest war ever fought. Yet it was George Washington who made their achievements possible. So long as this Republic lasts, he will always stand first.

So will his Monument. It speaks to our birth and our growth. It was unfinished at the time of the Civil War, which was fitting, since Washington, a slaveholder, came from Virginia, a state that in 1861 had seceded from the Union. In his Republic only white men of Western European descent could vote. But in his person and his policies he was the Father of a Union that was expansive not only in its territorial possessions but also in its very being. In his Republic the Africans could be freed and put on the way to full equality. So too for women, Asians, Latin Americans, Eastern Europeans, people from the Middle East. We truly are the world.

Without George Washington it is difficult to imagine how any of this could have happened. The Mall that stretches out in front of the Monument has been the scene of controversy and persuasion, which is as it should be in the democracy he founded. There more than anywhere, our national discord has been on display and our national progress created. The women's suffrage movement was advocated there. There Martin Luther King, Jr., spoke the words that above all others led the way to civil rights for African Americans and all other Americans: "I have a dream." There citizens gathered in uncountable numbers to protest the Vietnam War—something that could only happen in George Washington's Republic.

All this and much more has taken place in the shadow of the Washington Monument. It is there that we all come together to protest and to persuade. It is there, above any other place, that we have the monument that stands for our greatest national strength, our democracy, and that symbolizes our greatest national pride, our unity.

2000: MILLENNIUM FIREWORKS FILL THE SKY OVER A SCAFFOLD-SHEATHED MONUMENT.

CHAPTER ONE

A Monumental Hero

The Revolutionary War, which began with a burst of patriotic pride, went on and on.

Americans grew weary of sacrifice. All that most people had to show for years of war were

high prices and untended farms abandoned by Minute Men farmers—or harvested by

foraging soldiers. But everyone had George Washington, a man they called the Roman

Hero or the Grecian God, a man of whom they sang: "Huzza, huzza, huzza—for War and

Washington!" He was the Revolution and the Nation. They called him "the Soldier of

America." A German-language almanac hailed him as *Des Landes Vater,* the Father of His

Country, and that title quickly caught on. Somehow he transformed a ragged, untrained horde

into the Continental Army. Somehow he led his troops to victory, losing more battles than

circa 1785: TERRA-COTTA BUST FROM LIFE MASK BY JEAN ANTOINE HOUDON.

he won, but never losing the adoration of America.

When the war was won, admirers in Philadelphia hung a banner celebrating his thirteen virtues: wisdom, justice, strength, temperance, faith, charity, hope, courage, religion, love, policy, friendship, and constancy. It was the beginning of a hero worship unlike any the nation was ever to know again. Drawings and paintings portrayed him as majestic. At six feet three-and-a-half inches tall, he towered over most Americans. His physique, wrote Abigail Adams, wife of John Adams, summoned up the words of Dryden: "He's a temple Sacred by birth, and built by hands divine."

Educated Americans, schooled in Greek and Latin, saw in him the embodiment of such classic heroes as Jason or Aeneas or Ulysses. As a youth, he had gone into the wilderness on a quest, risked his life, saw death—and emerged prepared for more quests, ready for another mystic call of destiny. Although private about his religious beliefs, he did see himself touched by the divine. After escaping unhurt in a battle in his early hero-life, he wrote, "By the all-powerful dispensations of Providence, I have been protected beyond all human probability or expectation."

He was a warrior and, like most warriors, he believed that he carried into battle an invincible shield. "I had four Bullets through my Coat, and two Horses shot under me," he exulted after a battle in the French and Indian War. In another, he rode between two columns of panicky soldiers firing at each other instead of at the enemy. With his sword, he levered up the muskets, saving lives as he risked his own.

He could have been a sailor. In 1747, when he was fifteen years old, he was accepted as a midshipman in the Royal Navy, and was determined to fight for England, then at war with France and Spain. But his mother intervened and kept him on dry land. By then his father, Augustine, had been dead four years and he was being raised by his mother, Mary Ball Washington. She was so stern that one of George's playmates said he was "ten times more afraid" of her than of his own parents. When those same playmates later looked back on the boy named George, they described him as grave and dignified. He was the kind of earnest youngster who would copy by hand a book on manners: 110 "Rules of Civility and Decent Behaviour in Company and Conversation." They included, "Be not angry at table.... Contradict not at every turn what others say.... Labour to keep alive in your breast that Little spark of Celestial Fire called Conscience."

George Washington was born at Wakefield Farm, Westmoreland County, Virginia, on February 22, 1732 (February 11, 1731 by the Julian Calendar; today's Gregorian calendar was not adopted by England and her colonies until 1752). Little is known about his early childhood. (To fill this void, Parson Mason L. Weems, a preacher and a self-promoting bookseller, concocted the story that George chopped down a cherry tree and admitted it to his father, saying he could not tell a lie. In 1806 Weems slipped that tale into the fifth edition of his extremely popular and extremely inaccurate biography.)

At sixteen he went to live with his elder half-brother, Lawrence, owner of a Potomac River plantation he had named Mount Vernon after an admiral he had served under. George learned surveying and, still a lad, was given the commission to survey the vast Virginia holdings of Lord Fairfax. When Lawrence, suffering from an unknown ailment we know today as tuberculosis, went to Barbados in 1751 for his health, he took George

The General

A citizen soldier since his teens, George Washington donned a uniform so often that he almost invariably was painted in one (opposite). His military career began in the Virginia militia. He fought in the French and Indian War and retired with the honorary rank of brigadier general. He became a full general in 1775, when Congress appointed him commander-in-chief of the Continental Army.

G. Washington

with him. It would be the only trip George would ever make outside what is now the United States.

George, stricken with smallpox in Barbados, survived with a scarred face. Lawrence died the next year, as did his infant daughter, and George inherited Lawrence's property. So, in 1752, when he was twenty, George Washington became the master of more than a dozen slaves and a substantial landowner—some 4,200 acres, including 2,000 in the Shenandoah Valley. As a somewhat rough-hewn member of the Virginia gentry, he could camp in the frontier wilderness—sleeping under "one thread Bear blanket with double its Weight of Vermin"—dance quite well at a ball, lead the hunt in pursuit of the fox, and play passably well at cards and billiards.

He was also a major in the Virginia militia, and his reputation as a woodsman reached the ears of Lieutenant Governor Robert Dinwiddie, who was concerned about French incursions into Virginia territory. France, basing her rights on early French exploration, had long claimed the Mississippi River watershed and much of what was then western North America from Canada to Louisiana. In 1753 France extended her reach into the Allegheny River Valley, which Virginia also claimed. To defend their new possession, the French began to build a chain of forts from the lakes of Canada to the Ohio River. Dinwiddie gave Washington a letter challenging the French claim and told him to present it to the French commander, who was somewhere in the Ohio wilderness about 300 miles from the Virginia capital of Williamsburg. Washington was also to gather intelligence on French relations with Indian tribes in the area.

Bushwhacking on horses and then taking to canoes, Washington and his seven-man party reached an Indian village. There he conferred through an interpreter with tribal leaders, who professed to prefer the English over the French. At a French outpost, Washington dined with soldiers who, after "they dosed themselves pretty plentifully" with wine,

"soon banished the Restraint which at first appear'd in their Conversation, and gave a Licence to their Tongues. . . . They told me, That it was their absolute Design to take Possession of the Ohio, and by G—— they would do it."

After gathering "the best Intelligence I could get" from the tipsy Frenchmen, he met next with the ranking French officer in the Ohio Valley and showed him Dinwiddie's challenge. The Frenchman told Washington "that the Country belong'd to them, that no Englishman had a Right to trade upon those Waters; and that he had Orders to make every Person Prisoner that attempted it on the Ohio, or the Waters of it." The commander gave Washington's party provisions and sent them on their way.

"We had a tedious and very fatiguing Portage" down a nameless creek, Washington wrote in his journal, "several Times we had like to have been staved against Rocks, and many Times were obliged all Hands to get out and remain in the Water Half an Hour or more, getting over the Shoals. . . ." Washington, determined to get his information to Dinwiddie as soon as possible, struck out on foot with a companion. "French Indians," as Washington called them, appeared on their trail. One fired a gun at them but missed. They walked through the night, hoping that the Indians would not begin pursuit until daylight. Americans in the area recently had been killed and scalped.

The two men struck out for an unnamed river (possibly the Monongahela), planning to cross it on the ice. Finding the river unfrozen, they built a raft, which capsized in the swift-moving water. They made it ashore and journeyed on, hiking or riding through day after day of snow and rain to Williamsburg, where Washington reported to Dinwiddie. Mission accomplished.

Dinwiddie had Washington's report published at home and abroad. Washington's 7,400-word account of the seven-week odyssey gave him publicity in London as well as in the colonies. His life as a hero had begun.

In 1754 Washington, now a colonel, again headed into

the wilderness, this time leading an armed Virginia force of 300 men. On his way to France's Fort Duquesne in the upper Ohio River Valley, he built a stockade, which he called Fort Necessity, at Great Meadows, near what is now Confluence, Pennsylvania. He had not chosen a good site for his fort. It was on soggy ground about forty miles from a strong French force and far from his own supply lines. Wooded heights looked down on it from three sides. Despite the fort's limitations, he launched a surprise attack from it on May 28, pouncing on a French scouting party of about thirty men. Washington's men killed the French captain, Coulon de Jumonville, and nine others. Washington took the rest prisoner.

The French struck back on July 3 with 700 men, who surrounded the fort from the commanding heights. After an all-day firefight in a driving rain, Washington surrendered the waterlogged fort. The French disarmed the Virginians and said that since the English were not at war with France, they could return home. Washington acknowledged in writing that he was responsible for the *"l'assassinat"* of de Jumonville—an admission that France used in propaganda attacks on England. Washington later said he did not understand the word, which he took to be a French way of saying "killed," not "murdered."

Washington did not suffer from the incident, which led to war between France and England. The firefight and the "assassination" established Washington as a young hero. And, as British statesman Horace Walpole wrote many years later, "The volley fired by a young Virginian in the backwoods of America set the world on fire." For from that volley came the French and Indian War. The expensive war would drive France out of North America; England would levy taxes on the colonists to pay for the war; resentment over taxation would lead to revolution—and independence.

Although Washington had suffered what would be one of his many defeats in battle, Virginia welcomed him back as a victor. The House of Burgesses officially thanked

him. And London gazettes again hailed him as a hero. A remark he wrote in a letter—"I have heard the bullets whistle; and believe me, there is something charming in the sound"—found its way into one of the gazettes.

A FEW MONTHS AFTER HIS DEFEAT AT FORT NECESsity, Washington got his first lesson about civilian control of the military. Dinwiddie arbitrarily reorganized Virginia's militia into autonomous companies. Washington resented that, as well as an order making colonial officers subordinate to English officers. He resigned his commission in protest and took up life again as the squire of Mount Vernon.

Washington's skirmish at Fort Necessity had started an undeclared seven-year war that would determine whether France or England would control North America. In 1755 England sent General Edward Braddock to America with two regiments. Washington, although lacking a commission, joined Braddock's staff as a civilian aide-de-camp with the courtesy rank of colonel. While serving with Braddock, he wrote down many of the general's orders in a journal for future use. "My inclinations," he wrote a friend, "are strongly bent to arms."

In April 1755, ailing with fever, Washington marched with Braddock as he carved a road through the wilderness to take Fort Duquesne. Braddock's force—some 700 colonials and 1,400 British—crossed the Monongahela River and were only eight miles from Duquesne when 254 French and 600 Indians ambushed the forward column. During the slaughter, Washington had two horses shot from under him. Braddock, on his fifth horse of that bloody day, was mortally wounded and half his men were slain. Washington buried Braddock on the road he had made and had retreating wagons roll over his grave so that Indians would not find it and take his scalp.

"I escaped unhurt, although death was leveling my companions on every side of me," Washington wrote his

WASHINGTON CROSSING THE DELAWARE, from the famous painting by Emanuel Leutze. The expedition took place late in December, 1776 and

ed in the capture of Trenton by Washington's forces

Courtesy of The

A hero portrayed

In brave profile, Washington stands amid his men during the crossing of the Delaware River late on Christmas night in 1776. The painting, done in 1851 by German-born artist Emanuel Leutze, glorifies Washington in what would be an enduring icon in schoolbooks and on parlor walls. The flag shown was not designed until 1777, and Washington knew enough about boats not to stand up in one as crowded as this. But Washington, taking a great risk, did lead some 2,400 men across an icy river in a sleet storm—and surprised the foe, a garrison of Hessians at Trenton. Washington, who needed a victory to raise civilian and military morale, had relied on the boating skills of fishermen from Marblehead, Massachusetts. Before the battle Washington mustered his troops for a reading of Thomas Paine's *The American Crisis,* with its famous passage, "These are the times that try men's souls."

mother. Once more he was a hero in defeat. And the legend of Washington grew in the colonies. A Presbyterian minister suggested that Providence had preserved Washington "in so signal a manner for some important service to his country." A month after the battle, at the age of twenty-three, he was made the commander of all the Virginia troops.

After the battle under Braddock, Washington praised his Virginians for their bravery, but condemned the Redcoats who "broke, and run as Sheep pursued by dogs." In the months that followed, as commander of the Virginia troops, he imposed a harsh discipline on his men, hanging some for desertion, flogging many for failure to obey orders.

The war dragged on, becoming one of many theaters in a far-flung conflict that saw Spain allied with France and Austria with England in battles from the West Indies to the Philippines. Indians allied with the French singled out Virginia colonists. Washington and his few hundred men, drawing up a defensive line in the Shenandoah Valley, held off the Indians. But by the end of 1757, France and her native allies were winning the war, which meant France would get all of North America west of the Alleghenies.

Then, in 1758, Prime Minister William Pitt concentrated England's military forces under young, brilliant generals and told them to save North America. One of the generals, John Forbes, had Washington commanding 700 men from four colonies while Forbes led a force that defeated the French at Fort Duquesne. Renamed Fort Pitt, it became the site of a trading post later named Pittsburgh. To the north, English and colonial troops conquered Canada.

In the 1763 treaty that ended the war, France gave up all territory in North America east of the Mississippi River. Washington, with the honorary rank of brigadier general, resigned from the military, after having done his duty to "the country," as he called Virginia. His officers wrote of their regret for the loss of "such an excellent Commander, such a sincere Friend, and so affable a Companion."

During the war he had met Martha Dandridge Custis, a wealthy widow with two young children. They were married on January 6, 1759, and he became the adoptive father of Martha ("Patsy") and John Parke ("Jacky"). The next month, on his twenty-seventh birthday, he assumed his first elected office by attending a session of the Virginia House of Burgesses, the first representative governing body in America. One of his colleagues described him as being dignified, "with all the muscles of his face under perfect control," though "flexible and expressive of deep feeling when moved by emotions."

Although the House of Burgesses traditionally concerned itself with Virginia issues, the war against the French and their Indian allies had forced Virginians to think beyond their borders and ask questions about their status. Many had fought side-by-side with men from other colonies. And England was giving veterans of the war tracts of land. So if, say, a Virginian claimed land that was outside Virginia, would that make him another kind of colonist? And where did Parliament get the right to hand out American land?

Grumbling about distant rule by Parliament had begun in 1764 with passage of the Sugar Act. A year later came the Stamp Act, the first direct tax on the colonies; newspapers, almanacs, pamphlets, legal documents, along with dice and playing cards, had to bear purchased stamps that showed the tax had been paid. England's war with France had been expensive. England needed money, and the prosperous colonies, now free of threat from France, should understand that they had to pay for their redemption.

The Stamp Act produced an electrifying speech in the Virginia House of Burgesses on May 29, 1765. Patrick Henry, a brash young burgess, had introduced a resolution asserting that only Virginia had the right to tax Virginians.

The House generally supported criticism of the Stamp Act but did not like the tone of Henry's resolution. Angered by the opposition, Henry rose and, in the climax of a speech, shouted, "Caesar had his Brutus; Charles the First his Cromwell; and George the Third—"

"Treason!" cried the Speaker of the House.

"—may profit by their example," Henry concluded. Then he added: "If *this* be treason, make the most of it!"

The speech signaled more than any other words yet uttered that at least some Virginians were no longer content to be colonists of England. George Washington was among them, but he almost certainly had not been in the chamber when Henry spoke. He was probably back on his farmlands dealing with a drought.

Washington had been acquiring additional lands near Mount Vernon and in the Ohio Valley, buying tracts from fellow veterans. He was settling in as a squire, expanding and remodeling his mansion at Mount Vernon and dividing his plantation into five farms, each run by an overseer. Aware of tobacco's drain upon soil, he began growing wheat as well as tobacco. This helped to reduce his debts to English tobacco merchants. He was devoted to Martha and her children. The death of Patsy at the age of sixteen saddened him beyond consolation.

Over time in the House of Burgesses, Washington became a leader of a movement toward self-government. For nearly a decade, dissent grew. Then, in July 1774 he and fellow burgess George Mason co-sponsored the Fairfax County Resolves, which protested the British "Intolerable Acts." Those acts, passed in retaliation for the Boston Tea Party of 1773, closed the port of Boston; instituted a military government in Massachusetts and outlawed town meetings; put British officials above colonial law; and authorized the quartering of British troops in civilian dwellings, even though the Quartering Act had expired. The Washington-Mason resolves urged a boycott of British goods, offered support for Boston, and called for a meeting of what became the Continental Congress.

Three months after introducing the resolves, Washington was in Philadelphia as a delegate from Virginia to the First Continental Congress. He did not take part in the debates, and he was still hoping for reconciliation with the mother country. But his quiet, authoritative presence satisfied even the radicals. When fiery Patrick Henry was asked whom he considered the greatest man at the Congress, he replied: "If you speak of eloquence, Mr. Rutledge of South Carolina is by far the greatest orator; but if you speak of solid information and sound judgment, Colonel Washington is unquestionably the greatest man on that floor."

In the months leading up to outright rebellion, Washington was among the delegates to the Virginia Convention, called in March 1775 to produce Virginia's response to England's crackdown on Massachusetts. The words of fellow delegate Patrick Henry lit the flames of revolution: "Our brethren are already in the field. Is life so dear, or peace so sweet as to be purchased at the price of chains and slavery? Forbid it, Almighty God! I know not what course others may take, but as for me, give me liberty, or give me death."

EARLY ON THE MORNING OF APRIL 19 BRITISH TROOPS fired on Americans at Lexington, near Boston, killing eight and wounding ten. The British then marched on to Concord, where other rebels had gathered. At Concord—where, in Ralph Waldo Emerson's poem, "embattled farmers ... fired the shot heard round the world"—the rebels drove the British back to Boston. An army was assembling in Cambridge, Massachusetts. Men shouldering muskets were coming from Connecticut, New Hampshire, Rhode Island, and New York. They had no supplies, no staff, little ammunition.

Members of the Continental Congress were meeting in Philadelphia when word of the battle reached the city. Washington, a delegate from Virginia, attended the Congress in a military uniform, demonstrating Virginia's willingness to join New England in the fight. He was appointed chairman of every committee concerned with war. On June 14, John Adams rose to speak about "the state of the

Farewell to arms

On December 4, 1783, Washington says farewell to his officers at Fraunce's Tavern in New York City. Men wept like grieving children and uttered not a word, an officer recounted. That same month he submitted his military resignation to Congress, surprising many. King George III reportedly said that Washington's decision not to seize power made him the greatest man in the world.

colonies, the army at Cambridge, and the enemy." John Hancock, president of the Congress, expected to be named commander-in-chief of the patriots' army. But Adams spoke in favor of Washington, who, in humility, bolted from the room while, as Adams later wrote, "Mortification and resentment" showed on the face of Hancock.

No one opposed Adams' nomination. When Washington accepted the appointment, he said, "I beg it may be remembered by every gentleman in the room, that I this day declare with the utmost sincerity, I do not think myself equal to the command I am honored with." He would ask for reimbursement of expenses, but he would not take any pay.

"I am Imbarked on a wide ocean," he wrote his brother, "boundless in its prospect and from whence, perhaps, no safe harbour can be found." He hurried to Boston, taking over command on July 2. He found the British strongly entrenched. Scattered in outposts around Boston, with few supplies and little ammunition, was his Continental Army—14,500 men, untrained, undisciplined but, in his words, "able bodied, active, zealous in the cause and of unquestionable courage." They had already proved that on June 17 at Breed's Hill (now usually called Bunker Hill), where about 1,000 colonials held off 2,300 British troops until, exhausted and out of ammunition, the ragtag army fled, leaving behind 1,054 British dead or wounded.

Washington seized Dorchester Heights overlooking Boston, and began a siege that would last nearly a year. Finally, on March 17, 1776, the British evacuated the city. Washington then led his main force to New York City, where he found merchants supplying British ships in the harbor. Under his stern orders, the city finally joined the Revolution. Washington intended to keep New York at all costs. He told his troops that any soldier trying to hide from the enemy or retreating without orders would be shot.

On July 9, 1776, five days after the Declaration of Independence had been proclaimed, Washington assembled his main force in New York City to have the Declaration read to his men. He said he wanted them to know the meaning of the war. When British troops landed on Long Island in August, Washington made a series of tactical blunders and began a retreat across New Jersey into Pennsylvania. "Our situation is truly distressing. . . ." he wrote in a report to Congress. "Great numbers of them have gone off; in some instances, almost by whole regiments, in many by half ones, and by companies at a time. . . ."

Morale was at its lowest as 1776 was ending. Desperately needing a victory, Washington led his men across the ice-flecked Delaware River to Trenton on Christmas night, surprising a drunken Hessian garrison. The next day he captured more than 900 Hessians and seized Trenton. British regulars rushed to take the city. Outnumbered, Washington slipped away to Princeton, where he struck the British rear. Leading the attack on his horse, he shouted: "Parade with me, my brave fellows!" And when the British lines broke, he led the charge with another shout: "It is a fine fox chase, my boys!"

The well-publicized victories established Washington as a hero-leader and raised the morale of both soldiers and civilians. But 1777 saw the British occupying Philadelphia, and Washington defeated at Brandywine and Germantown. The defeats were not decisive because the British failed to destroy the Continental Army. And Washington was mastering a strategy: "Avoid a general Action," never "put anything at Risque," never be drawn into battle against superior forces. Above all, be a leader trusted by your men, even if you marched them barefoot through snow to a place in Pennsylvania called Valley Forge.

Of the 11,000 men who arrived in Valley Forge, nearly 3,000 were unfit for duty because they lacked shoes or clothes. Washington himself despaired in that December of 1777, wondering if his army would "starve, dissolve or disperse." He divided his troops into twelve-man squads who were to build their own log huts. Foragers roamed the countryside in search of grain and livestock. The dying began, and the dead were buried naked to bequeath clothes for the living. Dysentery, typhoid, and typhus spread from one filthy hut to another. Washington ordered five lashes for any man caught failing to use a latrine. Knowing the ravages of smallpox, he ordered the inoculation of every soldier.

With spring came the run of shad up the Schuylkill— men leaped into the stream with shovels and tree limbs to scoop up the fish. And also came the news that France had become an ally. Washington had prevailed. Valley Forge had been the ultimate test of loyalty. His men emerged as an army hardened, disciplined, and itching for a fight—"in excellent fighting trim," a Continental remembered, "as we were starved and . . . ill-natured as curs."

France's entry guaranteed victory, but it was long in coming. The war became a stalemate except for occasional clashes. In June 1778, Washington pounced on a British force withdrawing from Philadelphia and heading for New York. He ordered General Charles Lee to attack. Instead, he retreated. Washington dressed down Lee, swearing at him "till the leaves shook the trees," a soldier later said. Then, dismissing Lee, Washington took command. "His presence stopped the retreat," a staff officer wrote. ". . . by his own presence, he brought order out of confusiuon, animated his troops, and led them to success."

Now, for three long years Washington drew upon most of his thirteen virtues, especially constancy and hope. He preserved his army, with little support from a Congress of squabbling colonies. And he watched for the moment when, finally, he could hurl that army in a decisive blow. The moment came in 1781, when he raced south and, in a superbly coordinated operation with French land and naval forces, trapped the army of General Charles Cornwallis at Yorktown, Virginia. Cornwallis surrendered on October 19.

The surrender effectively ended the war, but Washington's work was far from done. Some of his soldiers, reacting to rumors that the army would be dismissed without being paid, fixed bayonets and surrounded Philadelphia's Independence Hall, where the Continental Congress was meeting. Washington sent troops to quell the demonstration, but Congress prudently moved to Princeton. Disgruntled officers, demanding their pay from Congress, were threatening to mutiny. Washington appeared unannounced before them, pulled a paper from his pocket, donned a pair of glasses, and began, "Gentlemen, you will permit me to put on my spectacles, for I have not only grown gray, but almost blind, in the service of my country." As tears of shame rolled down the weathered cheeks of his officers, he appealed to the "good sense of the Army" and urged them not to "sully the glory" they had earned. After his brief speech, he walked out. The crisis was over.

He himself wrote about the uneasy balance. Unless Congress, rather than the states, got the power to run the country, "the blood we have spilt in the course of an Eight years war, will avail us nothing."

Already his men were seeing him as the leader who in peace would be a general—or even a monarch. One colonel wrote to him, suggesting that he crown himself king, supported by "the universal esteem and veneration of an army." A shocked Washington replied that "no occurrence in the course of the War, has given me more painful sensations" than the colonel's suggestion. Instead of dictating this letter to a secretary, he wrote it in his own firm hand and made a file copy to show Congress, in case anyone ever thought that he had wanted a crown.

Washington, like his model, the Roman citizen-soldier Lucius Quinctius Cincinnatus, wished now to return to civilian life, as "a private citizen of America . . . under my own Vine and my own Fig-tree, free from the bustle of a camp and the intrigues of a court." He wished to "glide gently down the stream of life." But he was a hero and he had to be enshrined in memory. If he did not see that, members of Congress did. They must honor him with some kind of monument. And so began Congress' long and tortuous quest to immortalize General George Washington.

Cincinnatus at home

Washington, an admirer of the Roman citizen-soldier Lucius Quinctius

Cincinnatus, follows his legendary path by quitting soldiery and returning to

farming and family. In a Mount Vernon tableau, he sits with his wife and her

grandchildren, George Washington Parke Custis and Eleanor Parke Custis. He

treated them as if they were his own grandchildren by blood. In the background

is a servant, anonymous like many of master Washington's slaves.

CHAPTER TWO

A Search for Grandeur

The treaty ending the Revolutionary War had not yet been signed, and British troops still walked the streets of New York City when, on August 7, 1783, the Congress of the Confederation unanimously resolved that "an equestrian statue of General Washington be erected at the place where the residence of Congress shall be established." The statue was "to be of bronze—the General to be represented in a Roman dress, holding a truncheon in his right hand, and his head encircled with a laurel wreath. The statue to be supported by a marble pedestal, on which are to be represented, in basso relievo, the following principal events of the war, in which General Washington commanded in person, viz., the evacuation of Boston, the battle of Princeton, the action of Monmouth, and the surrender of York[town].

1796: UNFINISHED PORTRAIT OF WASHINGTON BY GILBERT STUART.

On the upper part of the front of the pedestal to be engraved as follows:

> "'The United States in Congress assembled ordered this statue to be erected in the year of our Lord 1783, in honor of George Washington, the illustrious Commander in Chief of the Armies of the United States of America during the war which vindicated and secured their liberty, sovereignty, and independence.'"

The statue was to be executed "by the best artist in Europe," under the supervision of the U.S. minister to the court of Versailles (as the ambassador to France was then known). To aid the artist, Congress was to ship to France "the best resemblance" of Washington "that can be procured." This resolution, brought forth by a Congress operating under the pre-Constitution Articles of Confederation, is the ancestor of all the other resolutions of all the other Congresses down the decades— resolutions that ultimately produced the Washington Monument.

The equestrian statue proposed in 1783 had an historic echo, for in 1776 the Sons of Liberty in New York had celebrated the Declaration of Independence by toppling an equestrian statue of George III. Now Congress wanted an equestrian statue of the general who had defeated the king. And there was another hint of a yearning for royalty: An American cannonball had propitiously ripped through a portrait of George III during the battle of Princeton. Patriots replaced the king with a portrait of Washington, as if sensing that he would be a kind of American king.

He certainly had the stature of a king, as many people remarked. At better than six feet tall, he towered over most of his soldiers. An aide described his head as "well shaped ... gracefully poised on a superb neck," with "a large and straight" nose, "blue grey penetrating eyes," high cheek bones and a large mouth. He was "at all times composed and dignified...." Benjamin Rush, a prominent Philadelphia physician, said: "There is not a king in Europe that would not look like a *valet de chambre* by his side."

Like a king, Washington was an icon. Artists created images of him that portrayed him as a symbol—in oils and marble, in life mask and profile shadow-pictures. What he symbolized evolved from patriot to warrior to victor to president and, ultimately, to nationhood. He begins his iconic career as a portrait and concludes it as a pure white, mystical obelisk. How this all came about is a saga that entwines the heroic deeds of Washington with the history of his nation and the inconstant Congress that professed to honor his memory.

Throughout the Revolutionary War, Americans, who had grown accustomed to seeing images of King George III, now saw far more of General George Washington as icons changed. Washington's stern, paternal face looked out from almanacs, children's primers, gazettes, broadsides, playing cards, and books, including Noah Webster's best-seller, *The American Spelling Book.* For two decades, an engraving attributed to Paul Revere appeared in editions of almanacs and the most popular schoolbook, *The New-England Primer.*

BUT THE STATUE THAT CONGRESS HAD DESCRIBED SO thoroughly had to wait because Congress had many other concerns, the chief one being how to govern quarrelsome states. Each one issued its own paper money, which rarely was recognized outside its own borders. Nine had their own navies to guard their coasts from out-of-state trespassers and to enforce economic reprisals against each other. James Madison said that Virginia, confronting both North Carolina and South Carolina, was "a patient bleeding at both arms." Massachusetts raised an army to quell Daniel Shays' farmer rebellion against state tax collectors. "We are fast verging on anarchy and confusion!" Washington wrote when he heard about the rebellion.

Back in Mount Vernon in his Cincinnatus role, Washington had learned his own lesson in interstate problems when he began a commercial enterprise, the Patowmack Company, to improve navigation on the Potomac River by building a canal system. He wanted to link the thirteen colonies to the rapidly populating frontier, binding "those people to us by a chain which never can be broken." He met with representatives of Maryland and Virginia, and he quickly saw that a two-state meeting was not enough. At his urging, the Virginia legislature invited all the states to review matters of common interest about trade and commerce. In September 1786, five states sent representatives to what was called the Annapolis Convention.

Boldly going far beyond the mandate of the convention, the delegates approved a resolution to meet in May 1787 in Philadelphia "to take into consideration the situation of the United States ... to render the constitution ... adequate to the exigencies of the Union." That meeting, destined to create a true central government, would become the Constitutional Convention. And Washington, summoned to duty once more, would lead the Virginia delegation. He would be unanimously chosen to preside over the convention. Washington's status was changing from general to statesman. The statue of a triumphant warrior was becoming less appropriate. Cincinnatus was returning to the Forum in full majesty, but as a civilian.

One night, a group of delegates—all of them successful politicians in their own states—started talking about the General Washington they had known during the war. Several remarked on how aloof and reserved he had been, even around men he knew intimately. Gouverneur Morris disagreed, saying he could be as familiar with Washington as with any friend. Alexander Hamilton scoffed at Morris, saying he would buy a dinner with fine wine for a dozen delegates if Morris would walk up to Washington, slap him on the shoulder, and say, "My dear General, how happy I am to see you look so well." Mor-

Moving tribute

Hero with his toga drooping, George Washington in marble braves the outdoors on the grounds of the Capitol. The statue originally occupied the Capitol Rotunda, but Congress exiled the statue, by Horatio Greenough, to the grounds in reaction to public shock at Washington's nakedness. The half-clad hero was moved again in 1908, this time to the Smithsonian's Museum of American History, where it resides today.

ris accepted the dare and, at a reception given by Washington, did exactly what had been proposed. Washington responded by reaching up and pulling away Morris' hand and regarding him, wordlessly and icily.

WASHINGTON'S COMMANDING PRESENCE WAS especially familiar to four of the delegates who had served on his staff. Of the fifty-five delegates, thirty-two had fought in the Revolution. All the states sent representatives except Rhode Island (dubbed "Rogue Island" by some delegates). They met in the Pennsylvania statehouse under an agreement to keep all debate secret until the final results were known.

Washington rarely spoke during the long, hot summer of some 10,000 speeches. When he did speak, delegates listened intently. One day he held up a document that had been carelessly left behind by a delegate. Outraged, Washington reminded the delegates of the secrecy agreement, chastised them, and said, "I know not whose Paper it is, but there it is, let him who owns it take it." He threw the document on the table and left. No one claimed the document.

As at the Annapolis Convention, some delegates went beyond their instructions. The Congress of the Confederation had authorized only amending the Articles of Confederation, which created a loose association of independent states. Virginia, leading a movement to scrap the articles altogether, proposed a new government consisting of a judiciary, a legislature, and a "national executive," at first envisioned as a committee and then as "the president," with a seven- and then a four-year term.

During debates over whether the executive should be a committee or an individual president, Roger Sherman of Connecticut condemned the creation of a sole executive as "the foetus of monarchy." But fears of a monarchy were eclipsed by the realization that almost certainly Washington would be chosen as the nation's first president. His character was insurance against tyranny. "You must be president,

no other man can fill that office," Gouverneur Morris wrote to Washington.

For the Constitution to become valid, it had to be ratified by popularly elected conventions in each state; it would go into effect as soon as nine states had ratified it. Delaware became the first, followed by Pennsylvania and New Jersey. Georgia, Connecticut, and Massachusetts were next. As opposition grew strong in New York and other states, Washington threw the weight of his reputation behind what he called "An indissoluble Union of the States under one Federal Head." One newspaper said his words were like a statement "dictated by God."

During the ratification debates, Washington was bombarded with letters urging him to become president. He politely declined, saying he was back in Mount Vernon permanently. However, when the Marquis de Lafayette, the young French officer who had been Washington's comrade in arms, joined in the pleadings, Washington confided that he might have to change his mind. Washington saw a crisis coming for the new nation: Britain had not given up America. What it had not won by war, Britain hoped to get by intrigues fostered by spies and incursions along the frontier.

After ratification by the ninth state in June 1788, Congress declared that the new government would begin on March 4, 1789. In elections held earlier, electors from every state unanimously had chosen Washington to be the first president. He was not enthusiastic about his new responsibility. In a letter to a friend he wrote: "In confidence I can assure you—with the world, it would obtain little credit—that my movements to the chair of Government will be accompanied by feelings not unlike those of a culprit who is going to his place of execution."

Washington "bade adieu to Mount Vernon, to private life, and to domestic felicity" on April 16 and set out for his inauguration in New York City, the capital. On April 30, girded by a sword and wearing a brown suit of American-made broadcloth with eagle-adorned buttons, Washington

George Town, and FEDERAL CITY, or CITY of Washington.

A nation's pastoral capital

Architect Pierre Charles L'Enfant (right), a temperamental Frenchman, presented President George Washington with a grand design (left) for a national capital. His "plan wholly new" encompassed 6,100 acres. In this 1796 view from the heights of long-established Georgetown (above), Maryland's rolling hills still dwarf the Federal City—called Washington's City by some. Buildings in the distance are at the mouth of the Anacostia River, called the Eastern Branch on L'Enfant's plan. To the left a three-arch bridge crosses Rock Creek. The span, one of the capital's earliest public works, linked settled Georgetown with a Federal City barely more than a village. A visitor in 1806 complained: "The roads are never repaired; deep ruts, rocks, and stumps of trees, every minute impede your progress, and often threaten your limbs with dislocation…. The country adjoining consists of woods in a state of nature, and in some places of mere swamp…."

L'Enfant's enduring vision

Viewed from a satellite, central Washington (right) closely matches L'Enfant's plan from 1791. On his design of the city grid, he put an equestrian statue of George Washington where the White House and Capitol axes crossed (see "A," under References, below, and the corresponding "A" indicated on the plan). Instead of a statue, the Washington Monument eventually rose, slightly off L'Enfant's intended alignment. Both the President's House and the Congress House are where L'Enfant wanted them. The National Mall establishes a straight-line alignment for the presidential shrines, its 146 green acres bounded by the museums of the Smithsonian Institution and rows of elm trees. The Mall's boundary to the north, Constitution Avenue, appeared in the 19th century, a wide thoroughfare that replaced the filled-in Washington Canal.

OBSE... ...ory of the PLAN.

... several Grand Squares or Areas, of different shapes as they are laid dow...
... commanding the most extensive prospects, and the better susceptible of
... Objects may require. either use or ornament may
... devised, to connect the separate and most distant Objects with the principal,
... at the same time. Attention has been paid to the passing of those leading Avenues
... ...ience.
... East and West, make the distribution of the City into Streets, Squares, &c.
... certain given points with those divergent Avenues, so as to form on the
... which are all proportional in Magnitude to the number of Avenues

...be Streets.

... divergent one, such as the communication ... in the
... breadth, and thus divided,

GEORGE TOWN.

Road leading to the Canal at the lower falls distant 3¼ Miles.

Bridge

Road to Alexandria.

PART OF VIRGINIA

... true Meridional line by celestial observation
... ...house; this line he crossed by another line
... ...se lines were accurately measured, and made
... ...un all the lines by a Transit Instrument,
... ...nt, and left nothing to the uncertainty

REFERENCES.

A.   THE equestrian figure of GEORGE WASHINGTON, a Monument voted in 1783, by the late Continental Congress.

B.   An historic Column_ Also intended for a Mile or itinerary Column, from whose station, (a mile from the Federal house) all distances of places through the Continent, are to be calculated.

C.   A naval itinerary Column, proposed to be erected to celebrate the first rise of a Navy, and to stand a ready Monument to consecrate its progress and Atchievments.

D.   This Church is intended for national purposes, such as public prayer. thanksgivings, funeral Orations, &c. and assigned to the special use of no particular Sect or denomination, but equally open to all. It will be likewise a proper shelter for such Monuments as were voted by the late Continental Congress, for those heroes who fell in the cause of liberty, and for such others as may hereafter be decreed by the voice of a grateful Nation.

E.   Five grand fountains, intended with a constant spout of water.   N.B. There are within the limits

30

1990

LINCOLN MEMORIAL   WHITE HOUSE   WASHINGTON MONUMENT   U.S. CAPITOL

1791

Today's Mall traces back to parkland in L'Enfant's plan, augmented by riverside land reclaimed in 1880s (dotted lines).

rode through the streets, past 30,000 people, to Federal Hall for his inauguration. A newspaper hailed him as godlike.

In a draft of his first inaugural speech, he adroitly dismissed fears of a dynasty by writing that "the Divine Providence hath not seen fit that my blood should be transmitted or my name perpetuated by the endearing, though sometimes seducing, channel of immediate offspring." But he dropped the remark, perhaps because it too poignantly revealed his realization that the Father of His Country could not be the father of children.

W ASHINGTON NOW WAS BOTH A SYMBOL OF democracy and a demigod for a nation that had no monarch or royal family to venerate. The word *venerate* would often appear in testimonials to Washington. "When I saw Washington," a delegate to the First Federal Congress would write in 1789, "I felt very strong emotions. I believe that no man ever had so fair a claim to veneration as he." The chargé d'affaires of France reported to Paris: "In more than one hundred gazettes, often very licentious, published daily in the United States, his name has constantly been respected; in an assembly composed of so many heterogeneous individuals as is that of Congress, he has always been spoke of with veneration."

He knew that his every move established a precedent, and he said he wanted these precedents "fixed on true principles." To follow the Constitution's charge that he seek the "Advice and Consent of the Senate" on treaties, Washington went to the Senate with a treaty with the Creek Indians. As the Senators made rambling remarks, Washington grew impatient and refused to show documentation about the treaty. After a "violent fret," he cooled down, but he vowed that he would "be damned if he ever went there again." Nor would his successors; when they sought Advice and Consent, they did not go in person to the Senate.

To oppose him was somehow to oppose America herself, a few associates muttered bitterly (and privately). Vice

President Adams complained about "the superstitious veneration" paid to Washington. "Instead of adoring a Washington," Adams said, "mankind should applaud the nation which educated him. . . . I glory in the character of a Washington, because I know him to be only an exemplification of the American character."

Congress still had not decided on the permanent location of the national capital—and thus there was no official place to put that equestrian statue authorized six years earlier, in 1783. Ultimately, though indirectly, it would be Washington who would choose the site for what would be not a statue but the Washington Monument.

The location of the capital, like so many other issues in Congress, involved a compromise between North and South: Congress would move from New York to Philadelphia in 1790. After ten years in Philadelphia, the government would move to a permanent site on the Potomac River. Congress gave Washington the power to find a capital site, "not exceeding ten miles square," somewhere along an eighty-mile stretch of the Potomac from its Eastern Branch to a western tributary, the Connogocheague—a name that inspired jokes about the wilderness awaiting Congress.

In January 1791 Washington proclaimed that the new capital would be along the Potomac River, from Georgetown, Maryland, to the north and Alexandria, Virginia, to the south. A riverfront village called Hamburg, also incorporated into the Federal District, was known as Foggy Bottom, which is still a neighborhood name. A Maryland newspaper promptly called the proposed capital "The City of Washington," although for a long time it would be known as the Federal City.

Under the act establishing the capital, Washington named three commissioners who were to buy or accept by gift the necessary land on the Maryland side of the Potomac. They called the Federal District the "District of Columbia" and endorsed the idea of naming the city within it after Washington. The commissioners were also to "provide suitable buildings for the accommodation of Congress and of the president, and for the public offices" by the first Monday in December 1800.

To design the capital, Washington commissioned Major Pierre L'Enfant, who had come from France in 1777 at the age of twenty-three to join the fight against England. In 1788 he had planned the transformation of New York's city hall into the first U.S. "Congress House" and the site of Washington's inauguration. Beginning in 1791, L'Enfant and Washington worked closely, and there is little doubt that the president encouraged a design that put the Congress House a long distance from what L'Enfant envisioned as the presidential "palace."

L'Enfant, temperamental and immune to compromise, exasperated Washington and Congress, which fired him. The city commissioners then launched a prize competition for the Congress House, soon to be called the Capitol. The winner was Dr. William Thornton, a Scottish physician and amateur architect. The use of a design competition established the precedent for the President's House and other Federal City structures, including, eventually, the Washington Monument.

On the grid of his city plan, L'Enfant had found a place, approved by Washington, for the equestrian statue that Congress had authorized in 1783: at the intersection of lines west and south of the Capitol and the President's House. L'Enfant's grid included a square for each of the fifteen states, which were to embellish them with "Statues, Columns, Obelisks, or . . . other ornament." This never happened, but an obelisk would someday rise over the City of Washington.

On September 18, 1793, Washington, who had been unanimously reelected to his second term, laid the cornerstone for the Capitol. He conducted the ceremony according to Masonic ritual, wearing a Masonic apron embroidered by the wife of Lafayette, who was also a Mason. Washington had long been a Master Mason, the highest rank in the Fraternity of Freemasonry.

MILLS'
STATUE OF WASHINGTON.

Washington gets a statue

Congress, which proposed an equestrian statue of Washington in 1783, commissioned one for the District of Columbia in the 19th century, inspiring this design by Clark Mills, a self-taught sculptor. He puts Washington on a horse terrified by the shot and shell of battle. The elaborate pedestal never became reality, but in 1860 the statue was unveiled at Washington Circle; nearby today is George Washington University. The face was modeled from a bust of Washington by Houdon (page 10).

For Washington, who had become a Mason at the age of twenty-one, Freemasonry was a rite of passage and an acceptance of principles that included belief in a Supreme Being and in the immortality of the soul. The inclusion of Masonic rites in a public ceremony attested to the power of Freemasonry, whose members included many influential men. The secrets and mystic rites of the Masons inspired unease among some Americans in the new republic, particularly because of the British origin of the organization. Masonic symbols abound in portrayals of Washington. In an engraving created in 1798, for example, he stands on a pedestal flanked by two obelisks. Because obelisks are of Egyptian origin, they showed the Masons' mystic connection with Egyptian stone builders—though Masonry dated only to the 18th century.

Declining a third term, Washington retired in 1797, after having said farewell to his fellow citizens—"Northern and Southern, Atlantic and Western"—urging them to "properly estimate the immense value of your national Union." *Union* had already become a fighting word. Washington and his central government were not universally admired. "Let his conduct then be an example to future ages. Let it serve to be a warning that no man may be an idol, and that a people may confide in themselves rather than in an individual," thundered the *Philadelphia Aurora*.

Washington returned, with great delight, to Mount Vernon. He drew up a new will that freed his slaves, numbering about 300, upon Martha's death. He had less than three years of retirement in his beloved Mount Vernon. On December 14, 1799, he died there of a throat infection. His last words were "Tis well."

Newspapers bordered in black told the nation of Washington's death. The formal day of mourning in the nation's capital of Philadelphia was December 26, but the grieving went on for months. In cities throughout the nation people found a way to unite in their mourning by staging and attending mock funerals. Women draped black silk on their dresses and wore mourning rings containing his portrait. Men donned black armbands. As late as July 1800 there were shortages of black cloth and memorial objects.

Engravings, often including obelisks, showed a woman in mourning—"America lamenting her Loss"—and an eagle weeping. One of the most popular had winged beings taking a robed Washington to heaven. Death had made him immortal—Father of His Country summed up the reality: Only he could have led the army that won the Revolution, and only he could have brought the new republic through its earliest days. He deserved lasting honor—a great monument. But what should it look like? Where should it be?

In Congress, Representative Henry ("Light-Horse Harry") Lee, who fought at Washington's side in the Revolution, wrote a memorial resolution with enduring words— "first in war, first in peace, and first in the hearts of his countrymen." But Lee could not get his fellow Congressmen to agree on how to back those words with something solid, such as granite or marble. Lee suggested a return to the equestrian statue of 1783. A Congressman from South Carolina moved to replace the horse with a mausoleum.

Architect Benjamin Latrobe, an enthusiast of Greek Revival style, suggested a "pyramid of one hundred feet at the bottom, with nineteen steps, having a chamber thirty feet square, made of granite" for a marble sarcophagus with four marble pillars. Congress, after much debate, accepted the Latrobe design. (He later would be chosen to finish the Capitol.) Mrs. Washington reluctantly agreed to deposit

The Winner

Robert Mills wins the Washington National Monument Society's competition with this design (opposite). He had designed a Washington memorial for Baltimore, completed in 1829. Appointed U.S. architect by President Andrew Jackson in 1836, Mills had designed several District of Columbia buildings, including the Treasury, Patent Office, and General Post Office.

SKETCH OF

WASHINGTON NAT.L: MONUM.T:

BY

ROB.T: MILLS,

ARC.T.

Washington's body in a Capitol mausoleum. The House in 1801 appropriated $200,000, but the Senate balked. The new century began with no monument, no mausoleum, and no money for either.

DECADES PASSED BEFORE A VAULT FOR WASHINGTON was built beneath the Capitol Rotunda. But not until the approach of the centennial of Washington's birth in 1832 did Congress appoint a joint committee to fill the vault, this time proposing that the bodies of *both* Martha and George Washington be placed in it.

Washington's descendants, however, would not move his or her remains from Mount Vernon. Even there Washington had not rested in peace. In his will he had asked that a new tomb be built for his body. No one got around to building a new brick tomb until 1831, after a fired worker, seeking revenge, broke in to steal Washington's skull. Instead he got the skull of Washington's nephew, Bushrod. After that, a new tomb was built, its gate was locked, and the key was thrown into the Potomac.

Congress ultimately agreed to have Horatio Greenough, an American neoclassical sculptor living in Italy, sculpt a heroic statue of Washington. Greenough portrayed a larger-than-life Washington stripped to the waist. The pose is based on the portrayal of Zeus by the Greek sculptor Phidias, who supervised the building of the Parthenon. Washington as a half-naked Zeus shocked the American public. One critic said Washington appeared to be "entering or leaving a bath." Two years later, the statue was removed from the Capitol Rotunda to the Capitol grounds. In 1908 it was transferred to the Smithsonian. It stands today in the National Museum of American History.

By the time the centennial of Washington's birth came and went in 1832, everyone concerned with honoring him realized that Congress would never erect a fitting monument. *The National Intelligencer*, a respected newspaper, after condemning Congress for its inaction, on September 24, 1833, announced a meeting at the District of Columbia's City Hall for "Those gentlemen who have expressed their desire" to join a group planning a monument to George Washington. From that meeting emerged the Washington National Monument Society and plans for a fund-raising drive. John Marshall, chief justice of the Supreme Court, became president of the society. During the mausoleum vs. statue debate three decades before, Representative Marshall had favored the mausoleum. Now Chief Justice Marshall put his prestige behind a monument.

Operating out of an office in the basement of City Hall, the society began a fund-raising drive, spreading the word through newspaper notices and appeals to church, business, and civic organizations. The limit on any individual donation was $1. In 1836, with about $28,000 invested by "gentlemen of prudence and elevated moral worth," the society launched a competition, open only to American artists, for designs of a monument that would "harmoniously blend durability, simplicity, and grandeur." One of the leaders of the society, former Librarian of Congress George Watterston, enthusiastically called for "the highest edifice in the world, and the most stupendous and magnificent monument ever erected to man."

Robert Mills, architect of Public Buildings in Washington, won the competition with a design that he described as a "grand circular colonnaded building ... 100 feet high, from which springs an obelisk shaft ... making a total elevation of 600 feet." The circular building, 250 feet in diameter, looked like a Greek temple. Above one doorway was a 30-foot statue of Washington in a Roman toga, in a chariot drawn by six horses and driven by Winged Victory. Mills estimated that his monument would cost $1,250,000.

In Chicago, prefabricated "balloon-frame" houses were being built in a week. The City of Washington did not move at that kind of speed. There now was a design for the Washington Monument, but not for twelve years—until 1848—would work even get started on it.

WASHINGTON, D.C.

Respectfully dedicated to the President and Citizens of the United States by the publishers, Smith & Jenkins, N.Y.

Portrait of what might have been

The Washington Monument, complete with pantheon, towers over Washington,

D.C., in this 1852 lithograph showing "Projected Improvements." They include,

at far left, a triumphal arch on Pennsylvania near the White House; a widened

Washington Canal with a suspension bridge linking parkland carriage drives.

At the far right is the original Smithsonian Institution.

CHAPTER THREE

The Monument Interrupted

At their first meeting in 1833, the citizens who founded the Washington National

Monument Society had only to look around to sense the long ordeal that they faced. The

cornerstone of the City Hall in which they sat had been laid in 1820, and thirteen years later

the building still was unfinished. So, for that matter, was the Capitol itself. British troops had

set fire to the Capitol in 1814, and that damage had not been fully repaired until 1819. It was

still topped by a copper-clad wooden dome. Congress would add wings and a gleaming iron

dome on its own building long before the Washington Monument would become a reality.

The City of Washington, then as now, was a creature of Congress. As soon as Congress moved

from Philadelphia to the wilds along the Potomac, its members enacted legislation denying

circa 1870 THE MONUMENT IS A STUMP, ITS FUTURE CLOUDED BY CONGRESS.

local government to the Federal City. Later, Congress provided the city with a charter that allowed the election of a city council, whose members elected a mayor. But when the society wanted a site for the Monument, its distinguished members had to go to Congress, not the mayor.

Congress responded in 1844 by erecting an obstacle in the form of Representative Zadock Pratt, chairman of the House Committee on Public Buildings and Grounds. Pratt came forward with a design by a Philadelphia architect that would create an American pantheon, honoring not just Washington but a platoon of patriots. This design centered on a "temple form" spacious enough to contain "the busts and statues of the Presidents of the United States, and other illustrious men of our country, as well as paintings of all the historical subjects which have or may be designed by our artists through ages yet to come." This art-jammed building was to be 150 feet high with a statue of Washington on its dome.

The House accepted the grandiose plan but the Monument Society did not. Congress then refused to act on the legislation needed to award a site to the society. Amid growing misgivings about the Mills pantheon-and-obelisk design that the society had accepted nine years earlier, the group formally awarded Mills $100 in 1845. A description of the plan, published in 1848, shows that in the pantheon were statues of the signers of the Declaration of Independence and heroes of the Revolutionary War. Thirty columns represented the states in the Union of 1845, and there was a portico with various sculptures. The obelisk was to bear, in relief sculpture, Roman imperial symbols and scenes from Washington's military career

THE SOCIETY AND MILLS HIMSELF SEEMED TO BE losing focus. In June 1845 he wrote a member of the society to point out that he could keep the proportions of his design but shrink it—and the cost. George Watterston, one of the first members of the society,

quoted Mills as saying that even if the Monument had to shorten to 300 feet, "succeeding Generations shall call the founders of this glorious work Blessed." Discussions about changing the design resulted in the disappearance of the pantheon, at least temporarily. The society, meanwhile, had abandoned its rule for a maximum contribution of $1 (the equivalent of about $15 today) and was collecting more money. Contributors, who included Mrs. James Madison, Mrs. John Quincy Adams, and Mrs. Alexander Hamilton, were given in return prints of Washington and the Monument. Large prints awarded after 1848 show two versions, each with an obelisk 500 feet high. On one side of the print is Mills' original design; on the other is a design that replaces the pantheon with a stepped pyramid bearing "names of the Statesmen and Heroes of the Revolution."

With about $87,000 on hand, the society in 1848 announced that work could begin—but where? If Congress did not donate land, the society threatened, it would find private land. And there was plenty of that. On a visit to America six years before, Charles Dickens passed through Washington. To describe it to his British readers, he advised them to imagine burning down the worst parts of London and building them up again "in wood and plaster." Then "plough up all the roads; plant a great deal of coarse turf in every place where it ought *not* to be ... make it scorching hot in the morning, and freezing cold in the afternoon, with an occasional tornado of wind and dust; leave a brick-field, without the bricks, in all central places where a street may naturally be expected; and that's Washington." Another English visitor, far less eloquent, called the city "a deserted village."

The best site for the Monument was the location that L'Enfant had selected for the equestrian statue. L'Enfant had envisioned a "vast esplanade" extending westward from the hilltop Capitol, intersecting in such a way that it would provide a view southward from the President's House. Here—on what would be called the Mall—would be the equestrian statue of Washington. But the Mall, so symmetrically grand in L'Enfant's plan, was a virtual wasteland and plans for the equestrian statue had long ago trotted off into the sunset. So had the notion of a mausoleum in the Capitol crypt.

The idea of Union was still shaky. As a representative from Georgia had said years before, if "the remains of our venerated Washington" were to be removed from Mount Vernon and civil war were to break out, then that precious relic would be "on a shore foreign to his native soil." Other representatives wondered what would happen if the capital moved again. Would Congress "carry with us the sacred bones of Washington," as a representative from Pennsylvania asked? So the Capitol tomb became a tourist curiosity and eventually a repository for the black-draped catafalque on which have rested those who, beginning with Lincoln, have lain in state beneath the Rotunda.

The society announcement in 1848 apparently spurred Congress to do something about beautifying the Mall while simultaneously ending the impasse with the society. Congress passed a joint resolution authorizing the society to erect the Monument "upon such portion of the public grounds or reservations within the city of Washington, not otherwise occupied, as shall be selected by the President of the United States and the Board of Managers of the Society."

The society chose about thirty acres near—but not exactly on—the L'Enfant site. It is about 350 feet east of the White House axis and 123 feet south of the Capitol axis on the L'Enfant plan. Surviving society records do not show why the society avoided the L'Enfant site. Because it is near the Potomac River, most historians have suggested that soggy ground forced engineers away toward ground better able to support the foundation of the Monument. But Pamela Scott, editor of Mills' papers, suggests that the choice "was due to both historical and aesthetic reasons rather than a pragmatic one." She points out that the Meridian Stone, erected by President Thomas Jefferson, occupied the center of the Mall. (The stone, intended as an aid

The invisible cornerstone

An artist shows Grand Master Mason Benjamin B. French leaning slightly to lay the cornerstone of the Washington Monument, on July 4, 1848. In reality, French had to descend eight feet; the cornerstone was in the foundation. Later work put it deeper. Today it lies more than thirty-six feet under the northeast corner of the Monument.

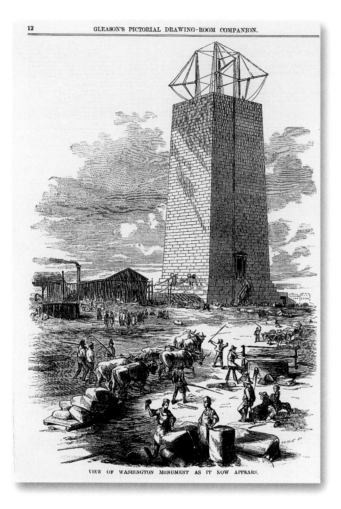

VIEW OF WASHINGTON MONUMENT AS IT NOW APPEARS.

A work in progress

The Washington Monument slowly rises in 1853. Oxen haul stones and stone cutters finish them. A steam engine in a shed provides power to stone-lifting cranes that jut from the top of the shaft. In 1854, dwindling funds will end the work, with the shaft at about 152 feet. The stump will stand for two decades as a symbol of an unfulfilled promise.

to navigation, was a chauvinistic American version of the British "first meridian" established at Greenwich.)

More important than the asymmetry was the fact that the site was near the river, which would serve as a cheap transportation system for the stones, sand, and lime needed for the Monument. The slight elevation gives the Monument a commanding location. Because the land was government-owned, the society had no worries about commercial development that would spoil the Monument's pristine isolation.

On April 12, 1848, the land was transferred to the society and, for the first time since 1783, events moved swiftly. The society hired Mills, at $500 a year, to act as on-site "architect and engineer." Mills, as architect of Public Buildings, was also watching over the construction of the Treasury Building, the Post Office, and the Patent Office (on the site L'Enfant had chosen for what he called the National Church). The society building committee set up a construction complex at the site—buildings for stonemasons and watchmen, rigs for hoisting stones—and a stone-handling wharf at the river's edge. A road connected the site to the river wharf, where stones were transferred from barges to oxen-hauled wagons. Contracts went out to quarries: blue stone, no less than sixteen feet long and seven feet thick, for the foundation; marble for the exterior from Thomas Symington's quarry in Baltimore. He arranged to deliver his marble by train. He soon found that the demands of the Monument overwhelmed the railroad, which did not have enough cars capable of carrying the massive stones.

Stonecutters had started using steam-powered machines to cut stones, but the building committee vetoed machines and insisted that the marble be cut and dressed by hand. At a time when public buildings were frequently built of sandstone, some would-be experts questioned whether marble was strong enough to support a 500-foot structure. Symington cited tests by the Secretary of the Interior showing that marble equaled granite in strength. Mills added an aesthetic consideration. A report by him and architect James Renwick boosted marble for its strength and for "the purity of its colour," saying marble was "better fitted to express the object of the structure than any other material."

Renwick, however, had chosen red sandstone for his Gothic-style building, the Smithsonian Institution, which began rising on the Mall a year after construction of the Monument started. Renwick's building offered another example of how long it can take to get something started in Washington. The Smithsonian building traced back to 1829, when an English scientist, James Smithson, had bequeathed his fortune to the United States for the creation of "an Establishment for the increase and diffusion of knowledge among men."

Mills supervised the foundation, which was excavated in the spring of 1848. Massive blocks of gneiss, or blue stone—some weighing six to eight tons—were lowered into the hole and bound by hydraulic cement and lime. "Every crevice of the stone is filled up with this mortar and grouted," Mills wrote. "The square or footing of this foundation for the obelisk is eighty feet each way, and rising by offsets or steps twenty-five feet high...."

When the foundation was finished, Mills had a committee of engineers, architects, and other specialists inspect and approve it. Then he had a shaft sunk in the middle of the foundation, to a depth of twenty feet to prove that a solid bed of gravel lay beneath. Six feet lower was water, a geologic fact that did not bother Mills.

THE CORNERSTONE WAS PUT IN PLACE IN A FOURTH of July ceremony grander than Washington had ever seen. Symington donated the stone, which weighed 24,500 pounds. Matthew G. Emery, a stonecutter who would later be elected mayor of Washington, did not charge for cutting and dressing the stone. He also cut a hole in the stone for a zinc box that would be a kind of time capsule. Into it went statistics on Washington (its population was about 50,000) and the United States (population 17,069,453 in 1840), coins and currency, a Bible, some sixty newspapers, reports of government agencies, and the first "Programme of Organization of the Smithsonian Institution."

A month before the ceremony, the Susquehanna and Baltimore Railroad transported the stone to Washington at no charge. The stone was transferred to a cart, which crossed the city toward the Mall, where the Washington Canal then flowed. While crossing the canal on a rickety bridge at 14th Street (about where that street now intersects Constitution Avenue), the cart broke through and plunged into mud.

Word of the accident reached the Navy Yard, which had special connections to George Washington. He had authorized the creation of the Yard and he had been a Mason, as were many workers there. Accompanied by Marine musicians, about forty men marched up Pennsylvania Avenue to 14th Street. Some 1,000 curious onlookers followed them in an impromptu prelude to the cornerstone ceremony. The men rigged two long ropes to the cart and hauled it and the stone out of the mud. Someone put flags and a live eagle on the cart and the men pulled it to the Monument site.

There had never been a Washington Fourth of July like this one in 1848. "Few left the city, while great multitudes rushed into it," the National Intelligencer reported. People from Baltimore, New York, and Boston took advantage of the half-price fares offered by railroads. The city awakened to church bells ringing and cannon firing salutes at the Navy Yard and the Arsenal. A wagon rolled by with a huge hogshead of water; on its sides, in whitewash, was "Fountain of Youth"—the contribution of a temperance society, competing with the barrels of beer rolling into saloons and hotels. Peddlers sold baskets of fruit and drinks in cooling clay bottles.

Then the sound of martial music blared, and down

Washington at war

The unfinished Monument stands like a ghostly sentinel of disunion behind officers of the Treasury Battalion, part of the defense force for Washington during the Civil War. Cattle grazed on the Monument grounds—part of the Union Army's "beef yard," a stockyard whose odors permeated the capital. The stench at times drove President Lincoln out of the White House to the Soldiers' Home on the outskirts of the city.

Pennsylvania Avenue came the parade, led by veterans of the War of 1812 and militia officers. Next came the carriage of ailing President James K. Polk, followed by his Cabinet, the justices of the Supreme Court, the diplomatic corps, members of the clergy—and a contingent of the Independent Order of Odd Fellows, a fraternal organization whose first U.S. lodge was named after Washington.

Congressmen came next, first the senators, then the representatives, including two who someday would be presidents themselves: Abraham Lincoln and Andrew Johnson (as would two other participants, Secretary of State James Buchanan and Vice President Millard Fillmore). Following Congress was a great miscellany of 4,000 Americans—governors and city officials, fraternal organizations and temperance societies, schoolchildren and firemen, and a large contingent of Masons, all wearing white gloves, dressed in black with white aprons girding their waists.

Near the end of the mile-and-a-half-long parade came open barouches. One bore Revolutionary War veterans who had served with the Father of the Country. In another were Mrs. James (Dolley) Madison, Mrs. Alexander Hamilton, and George Washington Parke Curtis. From another war just concluded in Mexico came Major General Winfield Scott, who less than a year before had been occupying Mexico City.

On the Mall, some 20,000 people had gathered. The lucky ones had paid a quarter to sit on seats under awnings or had arranged to arrive in their carriages. Tethered to a draped arch was the eagle that had greeted Lafayette in Alexandria twenty-four years before, when, at the invitation of Congress, he had made a pilgrimage to America. The eagle was a curious connection between the city and the French officer who had been wounded in the Revolutionary War as he fought alongside Washington.

Top-hatted Benjamin B. French, grand master of the Masons of the District of Columbia, laid the cornerstone by Masonic rites and spoke of Washington's character. French wore the same Masonic apron and blue sash worn by Washington at the cornerstone laying of the Capitol in 1793.

Robert C. Winthrop of Massachusetts, Speaker of the House, in an oration that lasted over an hour and a half, linked the Monument to "the illustrious Father of his Country" in a flourish of imperatives: "Build it to the skies; you cannot outreach the loftiness of his principles! Found it upon massive and eternal rock; you cannot make it more enduring than his fame! Construct it of the peerless Parian marble; you cannot make it purer than his life! Exhaust upon it the rules and principles of ancient and modern art; you cannot make it more proportionate than his character!"

It would be another while before the Monument reached to the skies. On July 4, 1850, two years after the gala celebration of the cornerstone, the society staged a fundraising event that was a flop. President Zachary Taylor presented a stone from the City of Washington for an interior wall of the Monument. Sweltering from the oppressive heat, he returned to the White House, where he consumed large portions of iced milk and cherries. That night he was stricken by cramps. He died five days later. (Modern physicians say that typhus, not a cherry overdose, probably killed him.)

The City of Washington stone was one of many such interior stones being contributed to the Monument in response to the society's campaign to get native stones from every part of the nation. Mills did his part by arranging for suitable heraldry and inscriptions for the state stones. But he had work elsewhere, and the stan-

Postal plea

With the Monument passing the 150-foot mark, the Monument Society launches a fundraising campaign (opposite), using the nation's postmasters as collectors. The leaflet shows the Monument as Robert Mills had envisioned it, complete with colonnaded pantheon. One such drive netted $2,240 from 841 post offices.

APPEAL TO THE COUNTRY
IN BEHALF OF THE
WASHINGTON

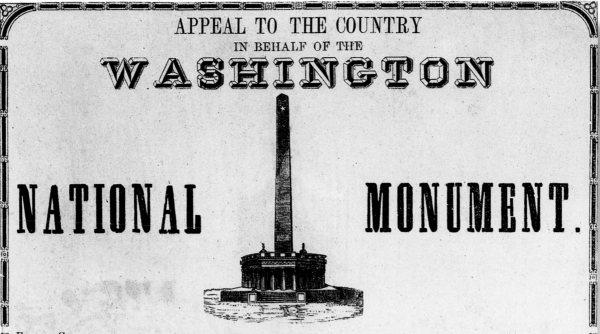

NATIONAL   MONUMENT.

FELLOW-CITIZENS:

The Monument so nobly undertaken by a few of our patriotic countrymen, to commemorate the worth and services of the Father of the Country, having reached 154 feet, of the 517¼ according to its plan, at a cost of about $230,000, needs your prompt and zealous support to raise funds, now nearly exhausted, to carry it on after the present month of June. Unless contributions are made this great National Work must be discontinued, if the Board of Managers, who render their services gratuitous, do not incur a debt upon their own responsibility. Is their patriotism to be so taxed, or shall this work begun in patriotism be a monument of national disgrace? Surely there are a sufficient number of noble hearted patriots in the land to prevent this.

Nothing but a small contribution from all, in proportion to their means, if only from a dime to a dollar each, is wanted for the completion of the Monument. The question is asked, will not such a contribution be made by every one? Will the people of this great country leave to a few the honor, after long years of trial and toil, of erecting a Monument worthy of the great and good Washington; or shall it be a National Monument from the whole people? That the Monument should stop short of one third of the plan proposed, no patriotic citizen can believe!

But the time for making contributions can be no longer delayed. Let every citizen ask himself, Have I discharged my obligation towards the Father of my Country; have I contributed my share to the Monument to be raised in his honer? If not, let him at once make his contribution, however small. Let it be made singly or by associations. But be sure it be made. Delay is hazardous to the great undertaking. The payment can be made to your Postmaster, or whoever may be most convenient to you, so that the duty of an American citizen be discharged. Every patriotic citizen surely will aid in forwarding the money received for the advancement of the great work. Will he not render that aid now?

The Board of Managers confidently trust that this appeal will not be made in vain.

OFFICERS:

FRANKLIN PIERCE, *President of the United States, and ex-officio President.*
ARCH. HENDERSON, *First Vice President.*
JOHN T. TOWERS, *Mayor of Washington, and ex-officio Second Vice President.*
THOS. CARBERRY, *Third Vice President.*
J. B. H. SMITH, *Treasurer.*
JOHN CARROLL BRENT, *Secretary.*

MANAGERS:

WINFIELD SCOTT,
N. TOWSON,
PETER FORCE,
W. W. SEATON,
W. A. BRADLEY,
W. W. CORCORAN,
P. R. FENDALL,
ELISHA WHITTLESEY,

JOHN W. MAURY,
WALTER JONES,
THOS. BLAGDEN,
WALTER LENOX,
M. F. MAURY,
T. HARTLEY CRAWFORD,
BENJ. OGLE TAYLOE.

dards of the stones were often ignored by the donors.

Mills was at work on another Washington monument, this one to be built at the site of Fort Necessity, where George Washington had been first tested in battle. Mills had designed a monument consisting of a fifty-foot iron column on a pedestal made of stones from all the states. The cornerstone was laid on July 4, 1854, and Mills died the following March. The monument was never completed.

THE IDEA OF CONTRIBUTING STONES FOR THE interior of the Washington Monument was extended to include such donors as fraternal organizations and foreign countries. Meanwhile, the building of the Monument went on, and the marble blocks began to give shape to something that for so long had been a dream. All went well until early 1854, when newspapers reported that the Monument had received a stone from Pope Pius IX.

Anti-Catholic, anti-immigrant zealots mobilized to keep the "Stone from Rome" out of the Monument. In a typical petition to the society, some "Citizens of New Jersey" said the inscription on the stone—Latin that translated to "Rome to America"—bore "a significance beyond its natural meaning." The pope sent the stone, they believed, as "an artful stratagem, calculated to divert the attention of the American people for the present from his animosity to republican institutions." The stone was stored in a stonemasons' shack on the site and, because of the threats, was guarded by a watchman toting a double-barreled shotgun loaded with buckshot.

As immigration increased in the 1840s, anti-foreigner, anti-Catholic societies sprang up throughout the country. One, the Order of the Star-Spangled Banner, formed in New York City, which had become a magnet for Irish Catholics fleeing the potato famine. Members of the order, inducted into secret rituals and practicing cultic discipline, were native-born Protestants. The anti-foreign groups organized openly as the American Party, which was popularly known as the Know-Nothing Party. The name came from the fact that, when questioned by outsiders, the secretive members answered, "I know nothing." The party's platform called for restrictions on immigration and the barring of the foreign-born from voting or holding public office. In 1854 the party, fracturing traditional political alliances, won control of the Massachusetts and Delaware legislatures, almost did the same in New York, and elected a mayor in Washington.

The stump of the Monument rose 152 feet into the midnight sky on March 6, 1854, when a group of men, later identified as the anti-Catholic Know-Nothings, surrounded the watchman's sentry box, wrapped a rope around it to keep him inside, and pasted newspapers over the windows that looked out upon the shed where the Vatican stone was stored. They broke into the shed, put the stone on a handcart, and took the block to the bank of the Potomac River. No one openly revealed what happened to the stone, but society officials said they believed the thieves broke it into pieces and probably loaded them into a boat and dumped them in the river. (*See page 91.*)

Shocked leaders of the Monument Society offered a reward and fired the docile, and possibly conspiratorial, watchman for acting "without effective remonstrance." They did not realize that the theft of the Vatican stone was only the beginning of Know-Nothing vandalism.

The society, which had been engulfed by fund-raising problems, had been sending out agents who collected contributions for commissions. Congress was suspicious of the work of the agents and, after an investigation by a select committee, reported that "not one cent of the funds received by the Society has at any time been lost by investment or otherwise." But the investigation, along with a general economic recession, had slowed contributions.

The select committee recommended that Congress contribute $200,000—the same amount that Congress had proposed for a mausoleum in 1801. The announcement was to be made on Washington's birthday, February

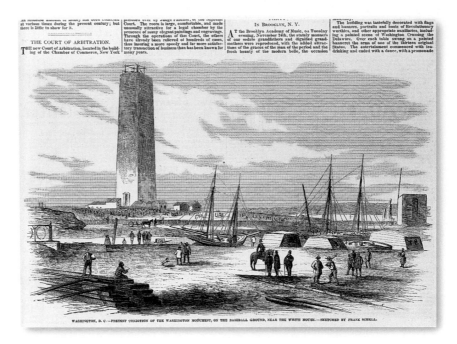

Ships ply the Washington Canal
in this 1874 view of the
Monument, once again awaiting
its fate at the hands of Congress.
Washingtonians also played
baseball around the long-
unfinished shaft, which had
become a familiar, if unsightly,
part of the capital's skyline.

WASHINGTON, D. C.—PRESENT CONDITION OF THE WASHINGTON MONUMENT, ON THE BASEBALL GROUND, NEAR THE WHITE HOUSE.—SKETCHED BY FRANK SCHELL.

22, 1855. But the night before, in a rigged election, a group of Know-Nothings seized control of the society.

The new proprietors of the Monument fired the superintendent and presumably all workers who were Catholics or foreign-born, and launched their own fund drive aimed at getting enough funds from "those born beneath the Stars and Stripes" to finish the Monument. The interlopers controlled the society for three years, adding twenty-six feet to the Monument, using marble blocks that the fired master mason had rejected. And, true to their name, they deliberately or carelessly disposed of many records that future historians would search for in vain.

The end of the takeover came with the end of the American Party. Millard Fillmore, who had assumed the presidency on the death of Zachary Taylor, ran as the candidate of the American Party in 1856, winning only Maryland. The party then died over the issue that was tearing the country apart, with antislavery Know-Nothings going to the Republican Party and proslavers joining the Democratic Party.

The demise of the Know-Nothings meant the restoration of the proper society board. Congress, although no longer interested in making a contribution, issued a charter incorporating the society. In a new fund drive the society placed contribution boxes at polling places across the country. But the election of 1860, which sent Lincoln to the White House, essentially ended the fund-raising. Americans who now turned their eyes toward the city named for Washington were not thinking about his Monument.

In Washington, the society gamely struggled on, confronted now by questions about the strength of the Monument's foundation. A young lieutenant of the U.S. Army Corps of Engineers pronounced the foundation sound. He then went off to the Confederacy, where he eventually became aide-de-camp to President Jefferson Davis.

When the Civil War began, the grounds around the Monument became a drill field and then a pasture for cows destined to become Union Army beef. On Washington's birthday in 1862, a Navy Yard rigger strung ropes on the Monument, climbed up hand-over-hand, and unfurled the Stars and Stripes. The flag was a symbol of the Union, but it flew over an ugly stump that symbolized a sundered nation.

Hope on the horizon

In a view from the Smithsonian Institution around 1879, the outlines of the National Mall begin to appear—and, finally, the Washington Monument once more is on the rise.

At the left is the Department of Agriculture with its symmetrical gardens. Next to the Monument are fishponds that supplied Washingtonians with shad, carp, and mosquitoes. The drained, recovered land would eventually provide sites for the Lincoln Memorial, the Reflecting Pool, and the Vietnam Veterans Memorial.

CHAPTER FOUR

Rising Again

With the Civil War ended and the Union preserved, the nation again could think about how to honor its first president. This phase in the long saga of the Monument began on Washington's birthday in 1866, when President Andrew Johnson called for resuming construction. "Let us restore the Union," he told a meeting of the Washington Monument Society, "and let us proceed with the Monument as its symbol until it shall contain the pledge of all the States of the Union." (Like all presidents since Andrew Jackson, Johnson was ex-officio president of the society.) Words, even coming from George Washington's latest successor, did not bring in the dollars that the society needed. Some money was trickling in. Masonic wives and daughters formed the Ladies' National Washington Monument

circa 1884: P. H. MCLAUGHLIN, OVERSEER OF CONSTRUCTION, STANDS AT THE BASE OF THE PYRAMIDION.

Association to raise funds. Several states also chipped in. Churches, patriotic groups, and fraternal organizations pledged donations, but they were pledges, not checks. Year after year the society saw the Monument slipping further and further into the future. Or into oblivion.

On the eve of the Civil War, the society had tried to raise funds by distributing collection boxes in post offices and making postmasters collection agents. During the four-month campaign the society collected only $2,240. At the end of 1859, the year that John Brown's raid all but guaranteed a war over slavery, the society had on hand $3,075. The Civil War would produce a chasm between an era of reverence for George Washington and an era of struggle to restore the Union. The Monument was lost in that chasm.

Before the war, from 1856 to 1860, the great orator Edward Everett spoke more than 120 times on "The Character of Washington," raising about $90,000 toward the purchase of Mount Vernon, the shrine of Washington. He is remembered most today as the man whose oratory was eclipsed by Abraham Lincoln at the dedication of the cemetery at Gettysburg.

After the war, it was the character of the assassinated Lincoln that hovered over a shattered nation. During the long travail of reconstruction, America tried to look forward, not back. A memorial to Washington was only an all-consuming matter for a small society in the District of Columbia. For the ordinary people of the nation, it was the recent tragic past that seized their souls. They were remembering a national nightmare, not a dream to honor Washington.

As the 1860s gave way to the 1870s, the society once more had to go to Congress for money, and Congress

Odd tops
As work was about to resume on the Monument, fanciful designs sprouted (opposite) out of the old stump. Many focused on ways to transform the plain shaft by topping it off with something sumptuous.

uncharacteristically seemed to respond quickly. On Washington's birthday in 1873, a select committee of the House of Representatives recommended that Congress appropriate enough money to complete the Monument by the Centennial of 1876. The select committee was reflecting the mood of the nation. During the Civil War the stump had been a reminder of national disunity. Now, as the nation prepared for its glorious Centennial, the stump, still standing amid the remains of cattle pens and a slaughterhouse, symbolized not only the discord of Civil War but also disloyalty to the sacred memory of George Washington.

Mark Twain in 1874 said it looked like a "factory chimney with the top broken off." Twain viewed the stump through a telescope because he did not want to get his shoes wet. "With a glass," he wrote, "you can see the cow-sheds about its base, and the contented sheep nibbling pebbles in the desert solitudes that surround it, and the tired pigs dozing in the holy calm of its protecting shadow."

The select committee, after conferring with the society, reported that Mills' pantheon was not needed for the completion of the Monument and could be built later. Mills had once said that without the pantheon the shaft would look like a "stalk of asparagus." Not so, said the committee confidently: "This rich and massive shaft, though simple and plain, would be a noble monument, worthy of the sublime character which it is designed to testify."

Once again, however, there was concern about the foundation. The select committee turned to Major General Andrew A. Humphreys, chief of engineers of the Army Corps of Engineers. He gave the mission to First Lieutenant William Louis Marshall, a bright West Point

St. Peters, Rome, 457 ft.

Strasbourg, France 465 ft.

Pyramid of Cheops, Egypt, 450 ft.

Spire, Landshut, Germany, 465 ft.

St. Stephens, Germany 441 ft.

Salisbury Spire, England 404 ft.

Capitol, Washington, D.C. 306 ft.

St. Pauls, London, 365 ft.

Washington Monument, Baltimore, 193 ft.

Bunker Hill Monument, Boston, 221 ft.

Drawn by Fred D. Stuart.

WASHINGTON NATIONAL MONUMENT.

Commenced, July 4, 1848.	Completed, shown by dark lines 174 ft.	40 Memorial Stones, built in the structure.
Cost, so far, about $230,000.	Proposed height, in dotted lines 485 ft.	83 Memorial Stones in the Lapidarium.
Required to complete the	Foundation, 80 ft. square; 8 ft. below the Surface,	Monument Grounds, about 30 acres.
structure, including the	and 17 ft. above the surface.	Monument Society chartered by Congress,
terrace, about $350,000.	Base of Monument, 55 ft. top, 56.55 feet.	Feby. 26, 1859, bill passed, Feby. 22, 1859.
	Terrace, Stone, 17 ft. above the surface.	
	Diameter of Terrace, 200 feet.	

Revised Plan of the Monument by Authority of the Society, Jno. B. Blake, Secy.

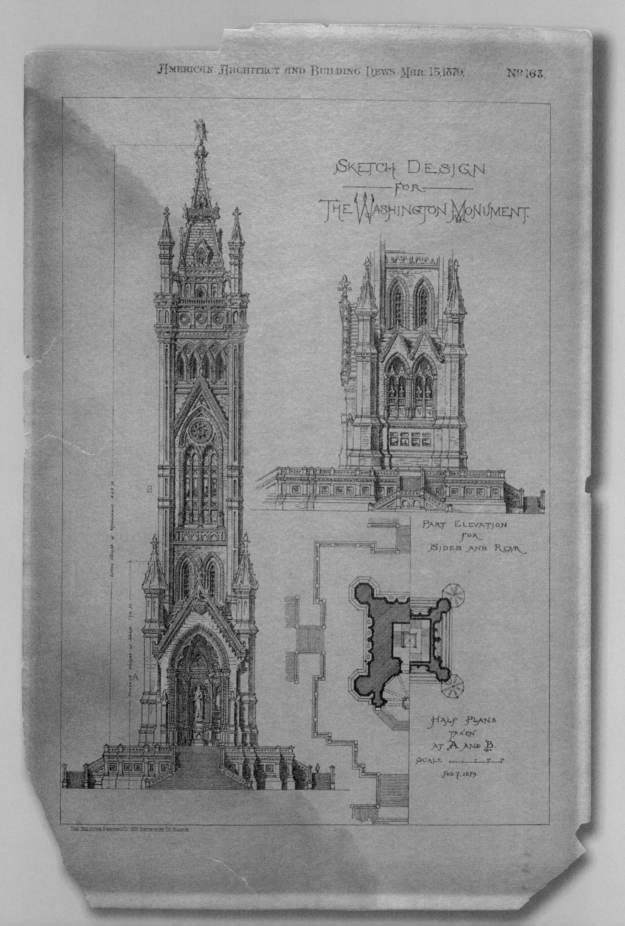

SKETCH DESIGN
FOR
THE WASHINGTON MONUMENT.

PART ELEVATION
FOR
SIDES AND REAR

HALF PLANS
TAKEN
AT A AND B.
SCALE
Feb. 7. 1879.

THE HELIOTYPE PRINTING CO. 220 DEVONSHIRE ST. BOSTON.

Victorian Dreams

Although the Washington National Monument Society long ago had selected a design submitted by Robert Mills, in the 1870s Victorian devotees were demanding a fancier Monument. Unbidden designs poured in, reflecting the era's yearning for excess adornment. A proper Bostonian submitted an English Gothic design (opposite) whose richly ornamented turrets rise to a tower topped by an angel. Something like a cathedral merged with the Taj Mahal (above, center) competed with a colossal edifice (above, right) that combined "modern French Renaissance" with "some of the better Hindu pagodas." Because Congress did not want to tear down the stump, it remained the interior of most designs. The original idea of an obelisk persisted in some proposals (above and right). The society was veering toward a Victorian finale until the U.S. Army Corps of Engineers, under congressional mandate, took over and, with soldierly pragmatism, got to work on an obelisk.

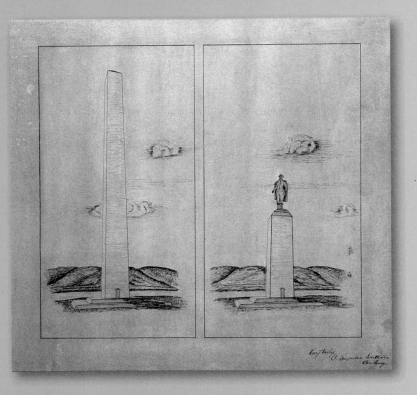

graduate who in 1908 would himself be chief of engineers. After what he admitted to be a "hasty and superficial inspection," Marshall reported that the foundation was as sound as his predecessor had found it in 1859. But, beginning what would be a steady assault on Mills' pantheon, Marshall recommended that the Monument be a simple shaft on a paved terrace, "presenting the appearance of a massive obelisk shooting vertically from the solid earth."

The select committee, recommending a $200,000 congressional appropriation to help the society resume building, said it would be possible to complete the Monument in time for the Centennial. Congress adjourned before a vote could be taken on appropriating the $200,000. And when the next session opened in January 1874, a reappointed select committee decided to look at the foundation again.

Back from a Corps of Engineers assignment in the West, Marshall launched a more thorough investigation of the foundation. Although he concluded that it was sound, he recommended that the Monument, which was then 178 feet high, rise only to a height of 400 feet. The ground beneath the foundation had already slightly settled under a pressure of 4.8 tons per square foot. A 600-foot structure (the 100-foot pantheon plus a 500-foot shaft) would put too much pressure on the substructure ground, he said. Marshall made structural suggestions that would drastically alter the shaft's appearance: Reduce the thickness of the walls from 11.46 to 7.3 feet. Put in a brick filling, bonded at 30-foot levels. Top the shaft with a roof of cast-iron plates supported by iron beams and rods rather than stone arches. Use brick for the upper 200 to 250 feet of the shaft, where the walls become thinner.

The select committee accepted Marshall's report, which recommended a shaft 437 feet high. A shorter Monument, the committee rationalized, "would be more graceful, and would be equally satisfactory to the American people." On May 1, 1874, the committee submitted its report to Con-

gress, urging swift passage of a joint resolution so that the truncated Monument could be finished in time for the Centennial. Nothing happened. On June 4, Representative John B. Storm, a Pennsylvania Democrat, rose to address the House. His speech was entitled "Washington National Monument: Shall the Unfinished Obelisk Stand a Monument of National Disgrace and National Dishonor?" The answer was yes. Again, Congress declined to finish the Monument.

DESPERATELY, THE SOCIETY AGAIN LAUNCHED A fund-raising campaign, hoping to get the American public behind a cause discarded by Congress. But support was eroding. The new questions about the foundation had led to questions about the design itself. In the decades since the original Mills design had been unveiled, popular tastes had changed. Victorian fussiness and ornate décor had come into vogue, and the plain appearance of the Monument seemed unequal to the grandeur it was supposed to convey. The influential *New York Tribune* attacked the Monument as "a wretched design, a wretched location, and an insecure foundation."

General Humphreys of the Corps of Engineers now got the jitters. He passed on Marshall's report to the Board of Engineers for Fortifications. The two generals on the board, both outranked and, of course, commanded by Humphreys, did not have to make any field tests to determine their commanding officer's apprehensions. They noted Marshall's 4.8-ton estimate and calculated that by raising the shaft to 400 feet, an additional pressure of 1.8 tons per square foot would result in "some subsidence." They recommended that no additional pressure be added—presumably dooming the Monument to a stumpy 178 feet (the society's 152 feet plus the Know-Nothings' 26 feet).

Humphreys handed this report to the committee and not only recommended another inspection of the foundation but also called for another design to ease the pressure on the substructure. He suggested that architects be asked to complete the Monument with "some suitable terminal, and possibly by additions at the angles of the column."

Architects and aesthetes of varying talents flooded the society with bizarre new designs reflecting ideas ranging from Gothic and Romanesque towers to a colossal edifice that combined "modern French Renaissance" with "some of the better Hindu pagodas." Joseph Goldsborough Bruff, an amateur artist and topographic draftsman, wrote to say that the abandonment of Mills' design would save the nation from "the infliction of a preposterous fancy." Bruff provided the commission with the dimensions of actual Egyptian obelisks and noted that colossal sphinxes usually accompanied them. His design made the Monument into a true obelisk rising from a plinth decorated with Washington's name and an All-Seeing Eye. Next to the obelisk stood an Americanized, eagle-headed version of the Great Sphinx. Surrounding the plinth was a thirteen-sided polygon paved in red, white, and blue. "From the roof platform of the plinth structure," he wrote, "patriotic addresses might be delivered on appropriate occasions. And, might not future Inaugural Ceremonies in propitious weather be appropriately sanctified from the same rostrum?"

Even an event as benign as the Centennial could cause trouble in the 1870s, when charges of corruption roiled through Congress and the administration of President Ulysses S. Grant. As a token of Centennial unity, a Congressman introduced a bill restoring full civil rights to the handful of ex-Confederates who had not been included in the general pardon of 1872. The proposal touched off a furious debate. James Blaine of Maine saw a chance to win support from anti-South diehards for his Republican presidential candidacy by offering an amendment excluding from the amnesty Jefferson Davis, president of the Confederacy and a man still revered by many Southerners. Blain's politicking split the Congress along party lines.

The City of Philadelphia, seeking Centennial recognition, had asked Congress to hold a joint session in the

WASHINGTON NATIONAL MONUMENT.

PLAN AS RECOMMENDED BY THE SELECT COMMITTEE OF THE HOUSE OF REPRESENTATIVES, IN THEIR REPORT MAY 1, 1874.

Congress almost approves

An obelisk "though simple and plain, would be a noble monument," a select committee of Congress decreed on May 1, 1874. Accompanying the committee's report was this drawing, which showed a 437-foot "rich and massive shaft" rising from a terrace adorned with fountains. The committee recommended that Congress appropriate funds to finish the Monument in time for the Centennial in 1876. But Congress lagged again in debates over design (a "blot upon architecture," said a senator) and concerns over the solidity of the foundation.

Starting at the bottom

The Army Corps of Engineers, now in charge of finishing the Monument, begins its task by digging down to the foundation, which will be widened and deepened to spread the weight of the Monument over a broader area. Workers will excavate under this old foundation—removing 10,334 cubic yards of earth—and pour in a concrete pad 13½ feet thick. The pad will extend 23 feet out from the previous edge of the foundation.

city where liberty had been proclaimed in 1776. The House genially consented, but the Senate, stubbornly refusing to agree with the House on any issue, rejected Philadelphia's request. The rejection shocked Philadelphia and most Americans. Editorial writers throughout the country thundered against the unpatriotic, anti-Centennial Senators.

John Sherman of Ohio sensed the need to show the Senate's appreciation of the Centennial and the Monument. On the Fourth of July, 1876, Sherman celebrated the Centennial by moving that Congress appropriate $200,000 toward resuming construction of the Monument. The Senate expected the House to cut the appropriation in half. But, to prove its patriotism, the House accepted the resolution. The bill passed unanimously in both the House and Senate, and President Grant signed the bill into law on August 2.

Americans got their Centennial but not the Monument. At the Centennial Exposition in Philadelphia, hundreds of thousands saw a new a symbol of freedom—a full-scale model of the arm and torch of the still-unfinished Statue of Liberty. The nation had gone far beyond the Revolution and George Washington. The Statue of Liberty would beckon new people to America, people seeking their New World. The largest immigration movement ever known was under way, and the Know-Nothings had faded into history. But, in a way, their vandalism lingered: The Monument still had not been built.

Congress had attached a string to the $200,000 for the Monument. The society could continue to raise funds, but it must transfer to the United States the Monument itself, the property it stood on, the stones await-

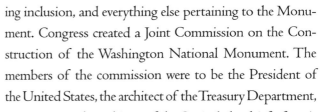

ing inclusion, and everything else pertaining to the Monument. Congress created a Joint Commission on the Construction of the Washington National Monument. The members of the commission were to be the President of the United States, the architect of the Treasury Department, the architect of the Capitol, the chief of engineers of the Army Corps of Engineers, and the first vice president of the society.

The very design of the Monument now was in danger. When the cornerstone was laid in 1848, Washington was hardly more than an overgrown village with wagon tracks for roads. There were no sewers and no dependable water supply. By the 1870s Washington was becoming the dual District of Columbia that exists today: the Federal City of government and the place where people lived.

"The citizen of the year of our Lord 1873 sees the dawn of the perfect day of which the founders of the Capitol so fondly and fruitlessly dreamed," wrote journalist Mary Clemmer Ames, author of *Ten Years in Washington.* "The old provincial Southern city is no more. From its foundations has risen another city, neither Southern nor Northern, but national, cosmopolitan." Ames also noted that "green pools which used to distill malaria beneath your windows" were gone because of a new sewer system, and the draining and filling of the Washington Canal, which became Constitution Avenue.

Congressional money was transforming the city, and Congress had made the Monument dependent upon that money. Some members of Congress even wanted to demolish the stump in favor of an embellished replacement. The society, foreseeing this possibility, had proclaimed that "all idea of surrendering the character of the Monument or allowing the structure, as far as completed, to be taken down, should be positively and emphatically disavowed." But now the society, which had only about $12,000 in its treasury, was no longer in control.

This became obvious when General Humphreys had independently called for another design. The commission tossed aside the pile of elaborate new designs and focused on the foundation, now beneath the ground for nearly thirty years. Thanks to the Know-Nothings, there were relatively few records showing early details of construction. According to Mills, an excavation near the Monument foundation revealed compact earth and then, twenty feet down, "a solid bed of gravel." He had been confident that the cement that bonded the blocks of gneiss, or blue stone, would itself "become as hard as stone."

The foundation was twenty-four feet thick, with eight feet above the ground. The visible foundation looked firm, but when Corps of Engineers workmen dug down, they found a mass of roughly laid rubble only partially held together by mortar. The foundation rested on what the engineers called a compressible bed. There was water at about thirteen feet, and below that a mix of clay, sand, gravel, pebbles, and boulders. This, they said, formed a strong natural platform.

The compressible bed consisted of a mixture of clay and fine sand, with the proportion of clay varying considerably, not only at various depths but also at each of the foundation's corners. The result was that one side of the foundation could compress its bed more than another side. The select com-

Stone upon stone
A stone leaves the hands of stone cutters (opposite) and begins its journey to the shaft. A steam-powered hoist carried the stones to cranes, whose arms thrust from the shaft (above). They lowered the stones into place.

mittee was contemplating the possibility of an American-style Leaning Tower of Pisa.

By the engineers' calculations, a shaft 600 feet high, with a breadth of 55 feet at the base and 30 feet at the top, would weigh more than 70,000 tons, pressing down 11 tons per square foot. Even at a height of 178 feet, the shaft was already inclining slightly toward the north and west. Cracks had appeared near the base. Joints between lower stones were chipped and fractured.

A second board of engineers, confirming the earlier finding that the shaft's weight already had produced "an excessive pressure for soils composed of clay and sand," recommended that no additional pressure be placed on the foundation. The first board called for stopping the shaft where it was—at 178 feet. The second Corps board reported that "the stratum of sand and clay upon which the monument rests is already loaded to the limit of prudence, if not indeed to the limit of safety." The report went on to say that the soil already had been compressed eight or nine inches and that the shaft was showing an "increasing departure from horizontality." There could be no justification for completion of the shaft with any design that would "load the underlying soil beyond 10,000 pounds per square foot."

The report of the board was completed in January 1877, but Humphreys appears to have rejected it, according to Louis Torres, a government historian, who in 1984 made a superb study of the Corps of Engineers' role in the building of the Monument. As Torres points out, Humphreys had taken control of the Monument and the paperwork of its construction.

The Army Corps of Engineers traced its history back to General George Washington, who appointed a chief engineer for the Army in 1775. The Corps' civilian history began with the enactment of the first River and Harbor Act in 1824. Because Congress made the Corps responsible for navigation and flood control on the nation's rivers, from then on the Corps found itself intimately involved with members of Congress in many pork-barrel dam and bridge projects. High-ranking officers like Humphreys were used to dealing with influential Congressmen. So when the Corps of Engineers stepped up the criticism of the Monument right after Congress had appropriated the $200,000, the society suspected a congressional plot.

The society claimed that the report was flawed and the foundation was not. Although now only an advisory body to the joint commission, the society demonstrated its influence by taking the dispute directly to President Rutherford B. Hayes, who a few months before had won the most controversial presidential election in U.S. history and had a seething Congress on his hands. Nevertheless, Hayes added the spat over the Monument to his agenda and, taking a personal interest, attended meetings in his role as ex-officio president of the society. The presidential hand of Hayes, a former Congressman, can be sensed, though not seen, plucking the Monument from the tangle created by Congress, the Corps, the society, and the joint commission (on which Humphreys sat while simultaneously running the Corps). Whatever the behind-the-scenes maneuvering, the result was that on June 14, 1878—America's second Flag Day—Congress passed a joint resolution authorizing $36,000 to reinforce the Monument's foundation.

A few days later, Humphreys made the most important decision ever made about the Monument: He put Lieutenant Colonel Thomas Lincoln Casey in charge of finishing it.

Casey was the perfect man for the job. He knew the ways of Washington and the ways of Congress. He had

Coming attraction

The slowly rising Monument looks down on guests of President Chester A. Arthur, who gathered on the White House lawn in 1882. When he became president after the assassination of President James A. Garfield, Arthur would not move into the White House until he moved out wagonloads of furniture and redecorated the rooms in Victorian style. That décor warred against the Monument's plainness. Arthur disregarded personal tastes on February 21, 1885, when he doffed his silk hat, put aside his doeskin gloves, and said: "I do now … in behalf of the people, receive this Monument … and declare it dedicated from this time forth to the immortal name and memory of George Washington."

completed the construction of the State, War, and Navy Department Building (now the Executive Office Building), had worked on the Library of Congress and the Washington Aqueduct, and had advised Congress on how to improve the ventilation of the House.

Casey quickly asserted his control, which was challenged by William Wilson Corcoran, a powerful Washington banker who was both first vice president of the society and chairman of the joint commission. Corcoran, infuriated by Casey's casual disregard, formally complained about Casey's behavior to no avail. Casey stayed in charge.

Casey settled the foundation controversy by determining for himself that the Monument could not be built on what was now beneath the shaft. He calculated that the combined weight of the foundation, the weight of the earth within and over the foundation, and the weight of the shaft itself totaled 80,378 tons—meaning that the earth under the foundation was being compressed under a pressure of more than five tons per square foot.

Casey ordered the building of the Monument stopped while he supervised a perilous undermining of the foundation. "Men whom I would be willing to trust for this work," he wrote, "are not to be found here." Looking for men "who do not mind the mud, darkness, and danger…," he sought out miners and personally recruited Baltimore workers who were excavating and making tunnels for a new water system.

In what Casey called "a delicate operation," the workmen dug beneath the eighty-plus tons, excavating pairs of tunnels from opposite sides of the foundation so there would not be an unequal strain on the structure. The digging went down fourteen feet beneath the old foundation.

Workers removed about 70 percent of the earth under the foundation and then filled the space with a massive concrete footing that extended thirty-five feet out from the Monument in each direction. They enclosed the stones of the old foundation in a concrete pyramid 100 feet square at its base.

As Casey described the completed foundation, it covered two and a half times as much area as the old foundation and was thirteen and a half feet deeper—only two feet above the high-tide level of the Potomac River. "The foundation," he said, "now rests upon a bed of fine sand some two feet in thickness, and this sand stratum rests upon a bed of boulders and gravel." Borings into this bed showed it was more than eighteen feet thick.

While work went on below, Casey contemplated what was to happen above. By now there was no chance that Mills' pantheon would be built. Congressional critics of the Monument wanted to somehow keep the stump, because demolition would not look like progress; simultaneously, they wanted the stump somehow enhanced. This congressional discontent with the Monument, together with the latest series of delays, inspired a new round of outlandish designs. One, by William Wetmore Story, an American sculptor who worked in Italy, would encase the stump in a "profusely enriched" marble "envelope" imitating "the Florentine Gothic of the Campanile of Giotto," topped by a marble pyramid and a statue of Fame. The joint commission was intrigued by Story's towering monument to Victorian excess and asked the society for an opinion. The society, abruptly abandoning its long allegiance to Mills, proclaimed Story's design "vastly superior in artistic taste and beauty" to Mills' plain old shaft. The new design, the society said, would "har-

Finished!

Scaffolding and the Stars and Stripes signal the completion of the Monument. The wooden pyramidal structure at top provides the platform for engineers to put the aluminum tip on the capstone. For the December 6, 1884, ceremony, members of the Washington Monument Society gathered on the lowest platform. A ladder led to the next level, where reporters and guests huddled.

The man who built the monument

Congress could not finish the Washington Monument, nor could the Washington Monument Society. But one man could—and did: Lieutenant Colonel Thomas Lincoln Casey of the U.S. Army Corps of Engineers.

The 100-ounce aluminum tip (opposite) that tops the Monument bears his name on its south face. On the east face he ordered the engraving of *Laus Deo*, Praise be to God.

Casey, in old Army jargon, was "born in garrison"—on a Lake Ontario fort where his father was a general. The Casey family homestead in Rhode Island was pocked with holes made by bullets during a Revolutionary War skirmish. Casey was naturally destined for the Army. He graduated at the head of his class at West Point and was assigned to the Corps of Engineers. During the Civil War he was in charge of constructing defensive works along the coast of Maine.

After the war, Casey was transferred to Washington, as assistant in the office of the chief of engineers. In keeping with the tradition of the Corps, Casey was more engineer than soldier. As the contractors for Congress, Army engineers under Casey built many government buildings in Washington. His no-nonsense approach won him the assignment to finish the Monument.

No one ever misunderstood Casey, a blunt man who knew how to say what he meant. Repeatedly, the society tried to get Casey to install a bronze plaque extolling the efforts of the society but ignoring the work of the Corps of Engineers. "The inscription . . . is misleading and unjust," Casey wrote his boss, the Secretary of War. It is "largely an aggregation of names . . . many of whom had nothing to do with the construction of the obelisk." The plaque was never installed. Although he retired in 1895 as a brigadier general and chief of engineers, he kept working as engineer in charge of the building of the Library of Congress. He died in 1896 on his way to the site.

monize conflicting opinions and give general satisfaction to the country."

Casey skillfully got rid of Story's medieval-Victorian fabrication by telling the joint commission that it would require slicing more than forty feet off the existing shaft. And, he added, with its buttresses and loggia steps and other fancywork, it would be too heavy even for the new foundation. The creation of that was costing more than the $36,000 Congress had appropriated for it. Earlier, Casey had asked for $99,102 more, had been turned down, but continued working. Now, using the Story interlude as a new opportunity, he asked again, and in June 1879 was given a $64,000 appropriation.

Admirers of the overly adorned did not give up. They asked, through the joint commission, for a terrace that would have bronze bas-reliefs portraying scenes in Washington's life. Casey did for a time entertain the concept of a terrace reached by double staircases and even told the commission that the terrace could be "capable of extensive and splendid ornamentation."

This seems to have been a temporary lapse, for Casey ultimately concentrated on building an unadorned shaft, the focal point of the original Mills design. Casey envisioned the shaft as an American rendition of the obelisks that guarded Egyptian temples. France had transported an obelisk from Egypt and raised it in Paris in 1836. Later, the Egyptian government presented obelisks to England and the United States. They were called "Cleopatra's Needles," though she had nothing to do with their history. The American obelisk would not be erected in New York City's Central Park until 1881. But, because of a popular interest in things Egyptian at the

Topping off

Ready for hoisting, the capstone (opposite) has had its top sliced off to accommodate the aluminum tip. On a rain-swept platform during the 1884 capping ceremony, Lieutenant Colonel Thomas Lincoln Casey holds his hat (above) as construction overseer P.H. McLaughlin readies the tip for Casey.

time, Casey undoubtedly had personal knowledge of obelisks.

Casey would get expert help on the subject from George Perkins Marsh, the U.S. ambassador to Italy and a classical scholar. Marsh had wondered whether the design of the Monument would follow ancient standards. He wrote to a friend, Senator George F. Edmunds of Vermont, who passed the inquiry along to Casey. Thus began a correspondence that had a profound impact on the future of the Monument.

Casey had only a general idea about the form of a true obelisk. Marsh had closely studied the thirteen Egyptian obelisks that had been brought to Rome as booty, beginning with the reign of Caesar Augustus (27 B.C. to 14 A.D.) The largest Roman obelisk, standing at the Piazza San Giovanni in Laterano, was 105 feet tall. Casey was planning a shaft 600 feet high. But Marsh converted him to the Egyptian proportion of ten times base to height. Since a width of 55 feet, 1½ inches already had been established, Casey planned for a height of 550 feet. (The final height would be 555 feet, 5⅛ inches.) A true obelisk, Marsh said, had a summit in the form of a pyramidion, the pointed pyramidal cap that forms the apex of an obelisk. The height of a pyramidion equaled the width of the shaft's base at an angle of 73 degrees. Marsh also strongly urged that Mills' pantheon be scrapped and that no decorative trim be festooned on the Monument. Casey, now a true convert, agreed.

Casey had been planning to "crown the shaft with a pyramidal roof of iron, which shall be 25 feet in height. This roof can be covered with hammered glass over some portions, to give light to the well of the monument." He estimated that his iron roof would weigh about 30 tons. Metal-and-glass was a modern, tested idea in 1878. The Crystal Palace, built in London for the Great Exhibition of 1851, had introduced architecture to iron-and-glass construction, and it seemed ideal to Casey. Not to Marsh. A roof like that, he wrote, would look "absurd."

Marsh, still educating Casey about obelisks, wrote: "The obelisk is not an arbitrary structure … its objects, form and proportions were fixed by the usage of thousands of years; they satisfy every cultivated eye, and I hold it an esthetical crime to depart from them." He conceded one modern adaptation: "There will no doubt be people who will be foolish enough to insist on a peep-hole somewhere." If that becomes necessary, he said, fit it with a stone shutter so it can be closed and present a uniform appearance.

Casey, who had struck up a friendship with Marsh, amiably agreed to redesign the pyramidion. He rejected the iron roof and replaced it with a Marsh-inspired pyramidion fifty five feet high. This gave the top of the Monument a seamless appearance like that of an Egyptian obelisk, which was carved from a single stone.

Casey turned to the task of laying stone to raise the shaft. He began by removing the inferior marble added by the Know-Nothings, reducing the height of the Monument to about 150 feet. Now the shaft was Casey's.

While keeping the exterior dimensions the same, he enlarged the interior to a thirty-one-foot square, with rounded interior corners for structural stability. The interior stones were granite, supplied from Maine quarries. The exterior stones of marble, he said in his specifications, "must be white, strong, sound … and must in texture and color so conform to the marble now built in the monument as not to present any marked or striking contrast in color, lustre, or shade…." But, as anyone who looks at the Monument can see, a striking contrast did result. Casey purchased some marble from a Massachusetts quarry, but he mostly relied on the Maryland quarry that had provided the marble used in the original 150 feet. He did not get a perfect match. The Maryland marble for the upper portion came from a different stratum. The result is the line at the 150-foot mark. Innumerable jokesters have told gullible newcomers that the line is the "high water mark" of a Potomac River flood.

An inner iron framework, produced by the Phoenix Iron Company of Phoenixville, Pennsylvania, is held together by I-beams and channel bars and anchored to the inner stones. The framework supports an iron stairway and platforms. The columns of the framework grew ahead of the layers of stone so that cranes could be attached to the columns and used to haul up the stones for the next layer. A steam-operated hoist, built by the Otis Brothers of New York, lifted the stones. It could raise ten tons at fifty feet a minute. The hoist's steel cables unreeled from a winding drum in a deep well beneath the ground floor. The hoist was powered by steam delivered in subterranean pipe from a marble and granite boiler house about 750 feet from the Monument. Casey had the idea of later turning the hoist into an elevator to transport visitors.

ON AUGUST 7, 1880, THE HOIST-TO-BE-ELEVATOR lifted Casey, President Hayes, and several other officials to the 150-foot level, where a crane had positioned the Monument's second cornerstone. (The first was below ground and part of the foundation.) Hayes scratched his initials and the dates on a coin and placed it on the prepared bed of mortar. Several others also placed coins, ending the short ceremony.

By the end of 1880, the shaft was 176 feet tall. By December 1881 it was 250 feet. A year later the shaft was 340 feet tall. Scattered among the interior granite stones were the memorial stones that the states, territories, foreign governments, fraternal organizations, and an assortment of other groups had been sending since 1849.

The year 1882 saw America entering a new age. On September 4, Thomas Edison threw a switch and inaugurated the Edison Illuminating Company by lighting up the

"Our matchless obelisk"

Thus did Representative John D. Long call the slender white shaft that finally became the Washington Monument on February 21, 1885, the dedication day. The ceremony had to be held on that day—a Saturday—because Washington's birthday was on Sunday, a day of rest and religion. On the snow-covered grounds, troops form in military review, Masons gather in their own group, and the pavilion near the base of the Monument fills with guests issued invitations (left) by Senator John Sherman, chairman of the congressional committee for the dedication. Included are officials of the three branches of government, diplomats, "a few ladies who had braved the Arctic weather," and "venerable citizens representing former generations" that had watched the long campaign to build the Monument.

NEW YORK, PUBLISHED BY CURRIER & IVES, 115 NASSAU ST.

Farragut Sq.   (NORTH WEST DIV.)   Scott Place   Louise Home   McPherson Space   Columbian University   Howard University
                                          Arlington House   Department of Justice   14th St Circle   Liberty Sq.   K St Market   Massachusetts Av.   Government Printing Office   B & O R.R. Depot
                    Corcoran Art Gallery   Lafayette Sq.   Foundry M.E Ch.   Ebbitt House   U.S. Patent Office   U.S. Post Office   City Hall Park City Hall   Pennsylvania Av.
                                                 EXECUTIVE MANSION   U.S.TREASURY   Riggs House   Pension Bureau   Census Bureau   Metropolitan Hotel   National Hotel
        Rawlins Square   WAR, NAVY & STATE BLDG.   (WHITE HOUSE)   Willard's Hotel   Washington Market   B. & P.R.R. Depot   Botanic
                            (SOUTH WEST DIV.)   The Presidents Grounds   Washington Monument   The Mall   Agricultural Dpt. Smithsonian Institute National Musuem   Jeffer
NATIONAL OBSERVATORY.   POTOMAC RIVER   Bureau of Engraving & Printing   LONG BRIDGE

THE CITY OF WASHI

BIRDS-EYE VIEW FROM THE POTOMAC - LOOKING N

Stanton Sq.   (NORTH EAST DIV.)
CAPITOL   Lincoln Sq.
                               Seward Sq.   U.S. Marine Barracks   Kendall Green
          (SOUTH EAST DIV.)   Navy Yard
                                             U.S. Arsenal
GTON.   EAST BRANCH OF THE POTOMAC
H.

COPYRIGHT 1882. BY CURRIER & IVES, N.Y.

Washington's new beacon

Tall and white, the Monument catches the eye in this Currier and
Ives lithograph, a new issue of an 1880 version that had the
Monument still unfinished. Ponds near the Monument will be
drained and filled in by 1887. The Capitol dwarfs the city, which
radiates out from it. The congressional greenhouse stands at the
foot of Capitol Hill. On the Mall are the tracks and train shed of the
Baltimore and Potomac Railroad.

Open for visitors

A stereoptican image shows "Endeavorers" entering the Washington Monument, an immediate

tourist attraction. Visitors began ascending in 1887. But not until 1888 did a steady stream of

tourists climb the stairs or ride the steam-powered elevator to the observation room.

offices of business baron J. P. Morgan. Electric cable cars traveled along State Street in Chicago at two miles per hour. The Brooklyn Bridge was nearing completion. Amateurs began taking snapshots with the easy-to-use Kodak camera.

The Washington Monument was not part of the new age. It was old before it was born, an icon of the 18th century still unborn as the 19th century neared its final decade. When would it be finished? Congress provided Casey with a steady stream of money, but progress was not steady because of delays in delivery of marble. A guidebook of 1883, which erroneously portrayed the future Monument surrounded by a terrace and an ornamental wall, said the Monument probably would be finished in a year. Not quite.

The shaft reached its 500-foot level on August 9, 1884. Mills had designed the shaft to have a taper of a quarter of an inch to a foot. (The walls attenuate from a thickness of fifteen feet at the base to a thickness of eighteen inches at the 500-foot level.) The tapering, which produces a graceful plane, was off by only one-quarter of one

degree from that used on the Egyptian obelisks. Casey was close to reviving the ancient geometry of obelisks.

The thinning of the walls of the obelisk eased the amount of pressure on the base and also decreased the weight of the next phase of the Monument: the pyramidion. A hollow pyramid fifty-five feet high, the pyramidion has two rectangular windows on each side. Originally, following Marsh's suggestion, they could be closed by marble-slab shutters that pivoted on bronze hinges. Since 1975 the window openings have been filled with bulletproof glass.

To lighten the pyramidion, Casey ordered the thickness of the stones thinned to seven inches, reinforced by interlocking stone ribs that he designed. At 470 feet these three interlocking ribs spring from each wall, forming a support for the pyramidion. Stonecutters dressed 262 pieces of marble to create the pyramidion, which is topped by a marble capstone. And that is topped by an aluminum tip whose tale tops off the saga of the Monument.

The story begins as the Monument was nearing 500

feet, and Casey was contemplating how to finish the summit. He knew that his obelisk had to have a protective topping that would also house a lightning rod. As he designed it, the copper rod would have a silvered tip protruding through the stone capstone. The rod would carry a lightning strike, via connecting rods, to the interior iron pillars, which would ground the charge in a well below the foundation.

Then he and Bernard Richardson Green, a civil engineer, developed the idea of making the cap entirely out of metal. Concerned about metal deteriorating and staining the top of the monument, Casey described the cap to William Frishmuth, a Philadelphia metallurgist, and asked for a pyramid cast in copper, bronze, or brass and plated in platinum. "Can you do it?" Casey wrote. "And at what cost?"

Frishmuth responded with a collect telegram and then a letter suggesting aluminum—a new, expensive metal never before used in American architecture. After a series of maddening delays, Frishmuth fabricated the largest piece of aluminum yet produced. It replaced the capstone's apex, which had been sliced off to accommodate the aluminum topper.

On a rainy December 6, 1884, at "2 o'clock and seventeen minutes past the meridian," Casey later wrote, "the cap stone was set by me and the Aluminum point secured ... thus substantially completing the walls of the obelisk." A battery on the White House grounds fired a twenty-one gun salute. An American flag unfurled. Cheers rose from the crowd far below.

The formal dedication ceremony came on February 21, 1885—the day before Washington's 153rd birthday and thirty-seven years after the laying of the cornerstone. Winds that "seemed to come from every point of the compass" whipped across ground covered with snow. An Army honor guard lined up for review by President Chester A. Arthur, who wore a fur-lined overcoat. He spoke more of Washington than of his Monument: "The faith that never faltered, the wisdom that was broader and deeper than any learning taught in schools, the courage that shrank from no peril and was dismayed by no defeat, the loyalty that kept all selfish purpose subordinate to the demands of patriotism and honor, the sagacity that displayed itself in camp and cabinet alike, and above all that harmonious union of moral and intellectual qualities which has never found its parallel among men...."

Robert Winthrop, who as Speaker of the House had delivered the cornerstone address thirty-seven years before, composed the major speech of the day. Too ill to speak, Winthrop had his address read by Representative John D. Long. "Our matchless obelisk stands proudly before us today," Winthrop had written. "The storms of winter must blow and beat upon it.... The lightnings of Heaven may scar and blacken it. An earthquake may shake its foundations.... But the character which it commemorates and illustrates it is secure...."

Grand Master Myron M. Parker presided over a Masonic rite similar to the one George Washington had conducted in the laying of the cornerstone of the Capitol in 1793. In the dialogue between him and the Deputy Grand Master, Parker asked, "Right Worshipful Deputy Grand Master, what is the proper implement of your office?"

"The square, Most Worshipful Deputy Grand Master."

"What are its moral and Masonic uses?"

"To square our actions by the square of virtue, and prove our work when finished."

"Have you applied the square to the Obelisk, and is the work squared?"

"I have, and I find the corners to be square; the workmen have done their duty."

They had indeed.

That night, fireworks flared at the foot of the Monument. One depicted Washington on horseback—a sparkling, ghostly reminder of the equestrian statue that had begun it all one hundred and two years before.

Writing on the Walls

In October 1849, little more than a year after the laying of the Washington Monument cornerstone, the Alabama state legislature authorized the governor to donate a block of Alabama marble to the Monument. Convict labor may have been donated, too, because records show that the block was placed on inspection at the state penitentiary in Wetumka. The stone bore a message: A UNION OF EQUALITY, AS ADJUSTED BY THE CONSTITUTION—an oblique reference to the constitutional issue of slavery that Congress was then fiercely debating. Thus began a U.S. history in stone, presented by the carved words on the Monument's inner walls.

When the Alabama stone arrived at the site, the Washington National Monument Society enthusiastically accepted and asked for stones from every state and territory. The society said the stones had to have simple inscriptions and be 4 feet long, 2 feet high, and 12 to 18 inches thick. But stones, often with ornate inscriptions or carvings, started arriving in various sizes. And soon more than states were sending their donations.

Because of the association between Masons and George Washington, the society asked for contributions from Masonic lodges throughout the country; fraternal organizations were also solicited. Money came in, and so did twenty-two Masonic stones, along with stones from the Odd Fellows, the Sons of Temperance, and other fraternal organizations. The surge of stones reflected the importance of Masonry and other fraternal societies in a mid-19th century America whose power structure was white, male, and Protestant. Later would come stones from a rising class: immigrants.

America was becoming a nation of the world. Stones arrived from China, Greece, Turkey, France, and England. In 1854, Commodore Matthew Calbraith Perry, after negotiating an historic treaty that opened Japan's ports to

GRAFFITI

CLIOSOPHIC SOCIETY, 270-FT LEVEL, EAST, MARBLE WITH SANDSTONE BORDER

Walls that Speak

Battered by time and vandals, the Cliosophic Society stone comes from a Princeton literary and debating organization founded in 1765. Repairers found Fallon's graffiti, still visible on a Monument wall, along with 193 memorial stones and two descriptive stones that came from states, fraternal groups, other countries, and 19th-century trade organizations. When the Monument was being completed in the 1880s, stones that had been waiting for decades finally were installed.

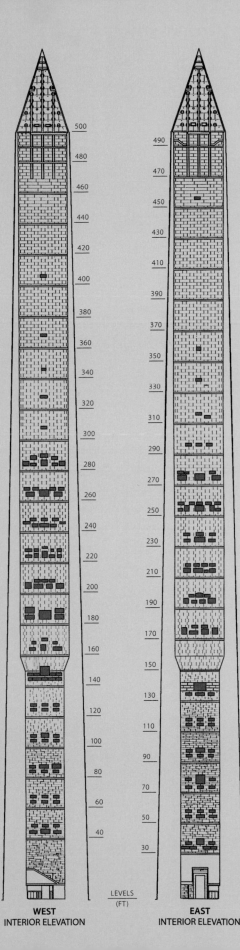

Stone locations

■ The location of the Monument's stones, shown on the following pages, are keyed to this cutaway. Under each stone photo is a line telling the kind of stone and where it is, by level and side. West and east elevations differ because of the zigzag path of the stairway.

western nations, stopped at Japan's Kingdom of Ryukyu (Okinawa). There he was given a gift—a stone for the memorial to "the great mandarin," George Washington. The Vatican also sent a stone. (See page 91.)

Many state stones bear the word *Union,* reflecting the struggle over slavery between supporters of a strong federal government and supporters of state rights. Indiana's stone: KNOWS NO NORTH, NO SOUTH. NOTHING BUT UNION. California's: YOUNGEST SISTER OF THE UNION. Louisiana's stone: EVER FAITHFUL ... TO THE UNION. Louisiana seceded in 1861.

Georgia's stone, which said, THE UNION AS IT WAS THE CONSTITUTION AS IT IS, arrived in 1851 and was inserted at the 50-foot level. But in 1852 the governor symbolically "withdrew" the stone (which was not removed) and sent another without the motto. That one (see page 93) finally was set at the 230-foot level after the Civil War. So was the Kentucky stone, which portrays its senators, Henry Clay and John J. Crittenden, each of whom tried to find a compromise to stave off war. KENTUCKY WILL BE THE LAST TO GIVE UP THE UNION says its stone, and in fact the state remained in the Union, while many of its men fought for the Confederacy.

Taciturn President Calvin Coolidge waxed eloquent when he dedicated New Mexico's stone, saying the monument "is built, stone upon stone, forming a solid and harmonious structure, just as America is composed of forty-eight states joined by the cohesive power of our Constitution."

Many of the earliest stones are at the lower levels because work on the Monument ended in 1855 at about 150 feet. Still girding the Monument is a line that shows where new construction began in 1876. That line also marks the reconstruction of the Union.

Souvenir-chipping vandals damaged many stones as they walked up or down the Monument. Since the 1970s, visitors have not been allowed to tread the fifty flights of stairs. The National Park Service plans to install windows and a recorded narrative in the elevator so that people can see and hear about some of the 195 stones they can no longer touch.

STATES

Every state has a stone in the Monument. (Hawaii, Kansas, Minnesota, Montana, Utah, and Wyoming were territories when they sent in theirs.) The most costly stone is Alaska's, carved from solid green jade. Arizona's advertises a tourist attraction: petrified wood. California sent two stones; the second was lost when the ship carrying it, the *Flying Dutchman,* went down off New Jersey. The stone, later recovered, was not set in the Monument. Delaware's is from a Revolutionary War battle that Washington lost. Hawaii's inscription translates as "The life of the land is perpetuated in righteousness."

ALABAMA, 40-FT LEVEL, WEST
MARBLE

ALASKA, 450-FT LEVEL, WEST
JADE

ARIZONA, 320-FT LEVEL, WEST
PETRIFIED WOOD

ARKANSAS, 30-FT LEVEL, EAST
BROWNISH LIMESTONE

CALIFORNIA, 120-FT LEVEL, WEST
MARBLE

COLORADO, 290-FT LEVEL, EAST
COLORADO YULE MARBLE

CONNECTICUT, 70-FT LEVEL, EAST
GRANITE OR DARK RED FREE SANDSTONE

DELAWARE, 30-FT LEVEL, EAST
GRANITE FROM BATTLEFIELD OF BRANDYWINE

FLORIDA, 60-FT LEVEL, WEST
NATIVE WHITE LIMESTONE

GEORGIA, 50-FT LEVEL, EAST
WHITE MARBLE

HAWAII, 360-FT LEVEL, WEST
CORAL SANDSTONE

IDAHO, 400-FT LEVEL, WEST
GRANITE WITH BRONZE FRAME

ILLINOIS, 50-FT LEVEL, EAST
LIMESTONE

INDIANA, 50-FT LEVEL, EAST
VARIEGATED NATIVE LIMESTONE

IOWA, 110-FT LEVEL, EAST
NATIVE LIMESTONE

KANSAS, 210-FT LEVEL, EAST
LIMESTONE

KENTUCKY, 230-FT LEVEL, EAST
GREY LIMESTONE

LOUISIANA, 40-FT LEVEL, WEST
PENNSYLVANIA MARBLE

MAINE, 30-FT LEVEL, EAST
GRANITE

MARYLAND, 80-FT LEVEL, WEST
BALTIMORE MARBLE

DESERET, 22-FT LEVEL, WEST
COLITIC LIMESTONE

MASSACHUSETTS, 70-FT LEVEL, EAST
QUINCY GRANITE

MICHIGAN, 210-FT LEVEL, EAST
SILVER AND COPPER

MINNESOTA, 220-FT LEVEL, WEST
RED SHALE OR RED PIPESTONE

MISSISSIPPI, 90-FT LEVEL, EAST
ITALIAN MARBLE

MISSOURI, 90-FT LEVEL, EAST
MARBLE

MONTANA, 220-FT LEVEL, WEST
MONTANA GRANITE

NEBRASKA, 220-FT LEVEL, WEST
LIMESTONE

NEVADA, 220-FT LEVEL, WEST
GRANITE

NEW HAMPSHIRE, 60-FT LEVEL, WEST
DARK BLUE GRANITE

NEW JERSEY, 70-FT LEVEL, EAST
NEWARK FREE-STONE FROM LITTLE FALLS

NEW MEXICO, 330-FT LEVEL, EAST
RED SANDSTONE

NEW YORK, 160-FT LEVEL, WEST
MARBLE FROM GLEN'S FALLS

Storied stones

Mormons hauled Utah's stone in an ox-drawn wagon; the trek to Washington lasted three months. "Deseret" is the realm created by Mormons in 1849 and unrecognized by Congress. Utah became a territory in 1850, a state in 1896. Michigan's metallic block cost the state $1,000. Mississippi, lacking native marble, offered sandstone and was turned down. So it imported one from Italy. Montana's stone arrived unengraved because the territorial treasury was broke. New Jersey notes two Revolutionary battlefields, Monmouth and Princeton.

NORTH CAROLINA, 100-FT LEVEL, WEST
WHITE MARBLE

NORTH DAKOTA, 350-FT LEVEL, EAST
RED GRANITE

OHIO, 90-FT LEVEL, EAST
LIMESTONE

*Mutilation,
explanation*

North Carolina dedi-
cated its stone on
Washington's Birthday
in 1853. North Dakota,
admitted as a state in
1889, did not get its
stone admitted until
1926. Oklahoma, admit-
ted in 1907, delivered
its stone 11 years later.
When South Carolina's
stone arrived in 1850,
vandals, apparently
reacting to the state's
strong anti-Federalist
stand, mutilated the
carved figures —even
though they are proba-
bly George and Martha
Washington. Tennessee
hailed the Union, but
seceded a decade later.
Utah, which entered
the Monument as a ter-
ritory (page 83), added
an "explanatory stone"
in 1951.

OKLAHOMA, 290-FT LEVEL, EAST
BLACK GRANITE

OREGON, 220-FT LEVEL, WEST
SANDSTONE WITH MARBLE AND SYENITE

PENNSYLVANIA, 180-FT LEVEL, WEST
WHITE MARBLE

RHODE ISLAND, 100-FT LEVEL, WEST
GRANITE

SOUTH CAROLINA, 60-FT LEVEL, WEST
MARBLE

SOUTH DAKOTA, 300-FT LEVEL, WEST
GRANITE

TENNESSEE, 230-FT LEVEL, EAST
NATIVE MARBLE

TEXAS, 290-FT LEVEL, EAST
GRANITE AND BRONZE

UTAH, 220-FT LEVEL, WEST
LITTLE COTTON WOOD CANYON GRANITE

VERMONT, 170-FT LEVEL, EAST
MARBLE

VIRGINIA, 80-FT LEVEL, WEST
JAMES RIVER GRANITE

WASHINGTON, 310-FT LEVEL, EAST
SANDSTONE

WEST VIRGINIA, 200-FT LEVEL, WEST
LIMESTONE

WISCONSIN, 100-FT LEVEL, WEST
FINE-GRAINED MARBLE WITH BLACK SPECKS

WYOMING TERRITORY, 220-FT LEVEL, WEST
REDDISH GRANITE

FOREIGN

The Ryukyu (Okinawa) stone brought back by Commodore Perry in 1854 mysteriously disappeared during the Civil War. In the 1980s, after getting an exemption to an 1899 regulation prohibiting any more foreign stones, Okinawa replaced its missing memorial. A mosaic salvaged from ancient Carthage appears on a stone misplaced in 1855. Found in 1958, it was never set in a wall. Wales hails "Our language, our country, our birthplace. Wales forever."

BRAZIL, 190-FT LEVEL, EAST
GRANITE

WASHINGTON BREMEN, 190-FT LEVEL, EAST, RED GRANITE
BRONZE

CARTHAGE, NOT INSTALLED
MARBLE

CHINA, 220-FT LEVEL, WEST
NOT IDENTIFIED

ALEXANDRIAN LIBRARY, EGYPT, 270-FT LEVEL, EAST
GRANITE

CHOW FOO, CHINA, 250-FT LEVEL, EAST
SLATE

FREE SWISS CONFEDERATION, 190-FT LEVEL, EAST
ALPINE GRANITE (HABKERN)

GREECE, 190-FT LEVEL, EAST
MARBLE FROM RUINS OF THE PARTHENON

SONS OF NEW ENGLAND (CANADA),
260-FT LEVEL, WEST, GREY LIMESTONE

OKINAWA, 310-FT LEVEL, EAST
NOT IDENTIFIED

TURKEY, 190-FT LEVEL, EAST
WHITE MARBLE

THE ISLANDS OF PAROS & NAXOS,
190-FT LEVEL, EAST, WHITE MARBLE

JAPAN, 220-FT LEVEL, WEST
FINE-GRAIN VOLCANIC ROCK

WALES, 240-FT LEVEL, WEST
BLACK GRANITE

SIAM, 190-FT LEVEL, EAST
FROM THE ROYAL QUARRIES

CITIES AND COUNTIES

Many donors ignored the society's request for stones of modest size. New York City's 8-foot-by-5½-foot stone alarmed engineers, who feared buckled cranes. New York refused to trim it. Philadelphia's measures 6 feet by 8 feet. Baltimore's 6-foot-by-6-foot stone, with a 39-word inscription, defied another request: simple messages. Frederick, Maryland, is similarly verbose. Newark, New Jersey, gets two stones, thanks to its Irish immigrants' Erina Guard. The Honesdale stone, donated in 1853 and set around 1889, was one of many that spent years in storage.

ALEXANDRIA, VIRGINIA, 280-FT LEVEL, WEST MARBLE

CITY OF BALTIMORE, 140-FT LEVEL, WEST GRANITE

BOSTON, 170-FT LEVEL, EAST GRANITE

CHARLESTOWN, MASSACHUSETTS 170-FT LEVEL, EAST, GRANITE

DURHAM, NEW HAMPSHIRE, 130-FT LEVEL, EAST GRANITE

FREDERICK, MARYLAND, 120-FT LEVEL, WEST WHITE MARBLE

HAWKINS COUNTY, TENNESSEE, 230-FT LEVEL, EAST BROWN AND WHITE MARBLE

HONESDALE, PENNSYLVANIA, 280-FT LEVEL, WEST LIMESTONE

THOMASTON MAINE, 100-FT LEVEL, WEST BLACK MARBLE

LITTLE ROCK, ARKANSAS, 90-FT LEVEL, EAST ROUGH GRANITE

LOWELL, MASSACHUSETTS, 250-FT LEVEL, EAST MARBLE

NASHVILLE, TENNESSEE, 40-FT LEVEL, WEST DARK LIMESTONE

NEW BEDFORD, MASSACHUSETTS 170-FT LEVEL, EAST, VARIEGATED GRANITE

NEW YORK CITY, 130-FT LEVEL, EAST MARBLE

NEWARK, NEW JERSEY, 260-FT LEVEL, WEST BROWN SANDSTONE

NEWARK, NEW JERSEY, 160-FT LEVEL, WEST BROWN SANDSTONE

CITY OF PHILADELPHIA, 180-FT LEVEL, WEST MARBLE

RICHMOND, VIRGINIA, 200-FT LEVEL, WEST GRANITE

ROXBURY, MASSACHUSETTS, 120-FT LEVEL, WEST
GRANITE

SALEM, MASSACHUSETTS, 170-FT LEVEL, EAST
GRANITE

STOCKTON, CALIFORNIA, 250-FT LEVEL, EAST
GRANITE

WARREN, RHODE ISLAND, 160-FT LEVEL, WEST
GRANITE

WASHINGTON, DC, 80-FT LEVEL, WEST
WHITE MARBLE

WESTMORELAND CO., VIRGINIA, 60-FT LEVEL, WEST
MARBLE

FIRE DEPARTMENTS

Social fraternity and political club, the 19th-century volunteer fire department was a powerful community organization. The firemen's growing importance in an urbanizing America is reflected in the number of their Monument stones. The Cincinnati Fire Division became the first full-time paid fire department in the United States in 1853, around the time the rival Invincibles and Independents proposed donating stones. They were probably inspired by George Washington's affinity to the Roman citizen-soldier Cincinnatus. Volunteers in Philadelphia—represented on two similar stones—trace their service back to colonial times.

FIRE DEPARTMENT OF NEW YORK CITY, 260-FT LEVEL, WEST
MARBLE

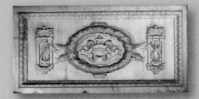

CINCINNATI COMPANY, 260-FT LEVEL, WEST
MARBLE

FRANKLIN FIRE COMPANY OF WASHINGTON, D.C.
30-FT LEVEL, EAST, MARBLE

INVINCIBLE FIRE COMPANY OF CINCINNATI, OHIO
80-FT LEVEL, WEST, LIMESTONE

FIRE DEPARTMENT OF PHILADELPHIA
250-FT LEVEL, EAST, MARBLE

ENGINE AND HOSE COMPANY OF PHILADELPHIA
250-FT LEVEL, EAST
MARBLE

ENGINE, HOSE, AND HOOK-AND-LADDER
COMPANIES OF PENNSYLVANIA, 250-FT LEVEL, EAST
MARBLE

MASONS

The first Masonic stone, at the 50-foot landing, came from District of Columbia Masons. Next to it is a stone from the Washington Naval Lodge, whose members helped pull the cornerstone to the Monument site. The stones abound in Masonic symbols, such as the open eye of God and the joined compass and square. There are also open Bibles and references to the 133rd psalm: "Behold, how good and pleasant it is for the brethren to dwell together in unity!"

MASONS OF ALABAMA, 140-FT LEVEL, WEST
ALABAMA MARBLE

MASONS OF ARKANSAS, 210-FT LEVEL, EAST
MARBLE

MASONS OF FLORIDA, 230-FT LEVEL, EAST
MARBLE

MASONS OF GEORGIA, 140-FT LEVEL, WEST
GEORGIA MARBLE

MASONS OF ILLINOIS, 140-FT LEVEL, WEST
MARBLE

MASONS OF IOWA, 210-FT LEVEL, EAST
GRANITE

MASONS OF KENTUCKY, 110-FT LEVEL, EAST
MARBLE

MASONS OF MARYLAND, 130-FT LEVEL, EAST
WHITE MARBLE

MASONS OF MISSISSIPPI, 210-FT LEVEL, EAST
SANDSTONE

MASONS OF NEW YORK, 110-FT LEVEL, EAST
DARK-COLORED MARBLE

MASONS OF OHIO, 110-FT LEVEL, EAST
MARBLE

MASONS OF PENNSYLVANIA, 180-FT LEVEL, WEST
MARBLE

MASONS OF VIRGINIA, 200-FT LEVEL, WEST
GRANITE

MASONS OF D.C., 50-FT LEVEL, EAST
MARBLE

LODGE NUMBER 21 NEW YORK, 130-FT LEVEL, EAST
MARBLE

MASONS OF LEBANON, PENNSYLVANIA
130-FT LEVEL, EAST, LEBANON MARBLE

MASONIC LODGE OF ROXBURY, MASSACHUSETTS,
170-FT LEVEL, EAST, GRANITE

ATHENIAN LODGE, TROY, NY, 160-FT LEVEL, WEST
MARBLE

WASHINGTON NAVAL LODGE, 50-FT LEVEL, EAST
MARBLE

MASONS OF ELLICOTT MILLS, MARYLAND
120-FT LEVEL, WEST, ROUGH GRANITE

LAFAYETTE LODGE, NEW YORK CITY
160-FT LEVEL, WEST, MARBLE

MASONS OF RICHMOND, VIRGINIA
200-FT LEVEL, WEST, GRANITE AND MARBLE

SONS OF TEMPERANCE

A movement that began in the early 19th century, the Sons of Temperance had a quasi-religious bent; members usually met in Protestant churches. By mid-century, as the Pennsylvania stone proclaims, the Sons called for lifetime abstinence rather than temperance: THE SUREST SAFEGUARD OF THE LIBERTY OF OUR COUNTRY IS TOTAL ABSTINENCE FROM ALL THAT INTOXICATES. Ulysses S. Grant, as a young Army officer stationed at an isolated post, joined the S of T but soon broke his temperance pledge. In 1876, as President, he authorized completion of the Monument, whose walls were studded with temperance stones.

SUPREME COUNCIL OF THE TEMPLARS OF HONOR AND TEMPERANCE, 200-FT LEVEL, WEST
MARBLE

SONS OF TEMPERANCE CONNECTICUT
130-FT LEVEL, EAST, MARBLE

GRAND DIVISION, ILLINOIS, 210-FT LEVEL, EAST
MARBLE

SONS OF TEMPERANCE OF OHIO, 110-FT LEVEL, EAST
MARBLE

SONS OF TEMPERANCE OF PENNSYLVANIA
180-FT LEVEL, WEST, MARBLE

SONS OF TEMPERANCE RHODE ISLAND
120-FT LEVEL, WEST, COMMON GRANITE

SONS OF TEMPERANCE NORTH CAROLINA
70-FT LEVEL, EAST, GRANITE

SONS OF TEMPERANCE OF VIRGINIA
70-FT LEVEL, EAST, MARBLE

INDEPENDENT ORDER OF ODD FELLOWS

Like the Masons, the Order of Odd Fellows attracted men renowned as pillars of their communities. The order traces its name to England in the 1770s, when upper classes remarked that common laborers who formed a fraternity were odd fellows. They pledge to visit the sick, relieve the distressed, bury the dead, and educate the orphans. The chain links on the stones stand for Friendship, Love, and Truth. The bundle of rods bound around an ax symbolized authority in ancient Rome. Philadelphia's large stone lists 72 lodges.

I.O.O.F. U.S.A., 200-FT LEVEL, WEST
MARBLE

EUREKA LODGE OF NEW YORK CITY
160-FT LEVEL, WEST, MARBLE

I.O.O.F. GERMANTOWN, PENNSYLVANIA
120-FT LEVEL, WEST, WHITE MARBLE

I.O.O.F. MISSISSIPPI, 210-FT LEVEL, EAST
LIMESTONE

I.O.O.F. NEW JERSEY, 60-FT LEVEL, WEST
RED SANDSTONE

R.W. GRAND LODGE OF INDIANA, 80-FT LEVEL, WEST
MARBLE

ODD FELLOWS OF KENTUCKY, 230-FT LEVEL, EAST
LIMESTONE

I.O.O.F. MARYLAND, 200-FT LEVEL, WEST
WHITE MARBLE

I.O.O.F. MASSACHUSETTS, 130-FT LEVEL, EAST
WHITE MARBLE

I.O.O.F. PHILADELPHIA, 180-FT LEVEL, WEST
HIGHLY VARIEGATED MARBLE

I.O.O.F. VIRGINIA, 100-FT LEVEL, WEST
MARBLE

ODD FELLOWS OF OHIO, 90-FT LEVEL, EAST
LIMESTONE

A ROMA AMERICAE

VATICAN, 340-FT LEVEL, WEST, CARERRA MARBLE

The case of the missing Vatican stone

Sometime after midnight on March 6, 1854, thieves stole one of the stones stored in a shed on the grounds of the Washington Monument. The stone, donated by Pope Pius IX, had been part of the ancient Temple of Concord in Rome. *The National Intelligencer* called the theft a "deed of barbarism."

Anti-Catholic Know-Nothings were blamed. Word circulated in Washington that the thieves had broken up the "Pope's Stone," as it became known, and dumped the pieces in the Potomac River. The stone was never seen again. Or was it?

Rumors persisted that pieces of the stone had been kept as souvenirs. Workers supposedly found the stone in 1927 while digging a utility trench at 21st and R Streets in Washington. The story went that a supervisor ordered them to cover up the stone and never talk about it

In 1959, the Right Reverend Philip M. Hannan, the auxiliary bishop of the Roman Catholic archdiocese of Washington, told a reporter for *The Washington Star* that an elderly woman had given him a crudely carved miniature of the Monument several years before. She said that her grandfather had told her that he had been one of the men who had stolen the Pope Stone and had carved the miniature from one of the pieces.

More years passed. Quiet efforts were made to replace the stolen stone. In 1982, the Right Reverend Hannan, then archbishop of New Orleans, presented to the Monument another gift from the Vatican (above), bearing the Latin inscription of the 1854 stone: A ROMA AMERICAE, From Rome to America.

SPECIAL

Some stones fit no broad category. The American Medical Association sent a beautifully carved stone; its figures were mutilated after installation. Stones came from bands of soldiers, from schoolchildren and teachers, from "tribes" of the International Order of Red Men, and from real Indians, the Cherokee Nation. Only 12 years before, the U.S. government had exiled the Cherokees to Oklahoma on the Trail of Tears.

COMPANY I, 140-FT LEVEL, WEST
WHITE MARBLE WITH SPECS OF MICA

AMERICAN MEDICAL ASSOCIATION
240-FT LEVEL, WEST, VERMONT MARBLE

AMERICAN INSTITUTE OF THE CITY OF NEW YORK,
130-FT LEVEL, EAST, OFF-WHITE MARBLE

AMERICAN WHIG SOCIETY, 130-FT LEVEL, EAST
MARBLE

ANACOSTIA TRIBE, WASHINGTON, DC
60-FT LEVEL, WEST, MARBLE

ENGINEERS OF THE SECOND DIVISION, VIRGINIA
140-FT LEVEL, WEST, GRANITE

BALTIMORE MARYLAND, 260-FT LEVEL, WEST
MARBLE

FROM BRADDOCKS FIELD, 240-FT LEVEL, WEST
CHESTNUT-COLORED MARBLE

BUFFALO PUBLIC SCHOOLS, 250-FT LEVEL, EAST
MARBLE

TOP OF THE STATUE OF FREEDOM ON CAPITOL
330-FT LEVEL, EAST, MARBLE

THOMAS CARBERY, 100-FT LEVEL

PROPRIETORS OF THE CINCINNATI COMMERCIAL
250-FT LEVEL, EAST, SANDSTONE

CHEROKEE NATION, 220-FT LEVEL, WEST
SANDSTONE

STONECUTTERS AND JOURNEYMEN OF PHILADELPHIA, 40-FT LEVEL, WEST
MARBLE

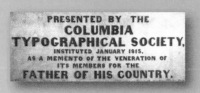

COLUMBIA TYPOGRAPHICAL SOCIETY
40-FT LEVEL, WEST, MARBLE

CONTINENTAL GUARD OF NEW ORLEANS
270-FT LEVEL, EAST, VARIEGATED MARBLE

DISCIPLES OF DAGUERRE, 280-FT LEVEL, WEST
MARBLE

DRAMATIC PROFESSION OF AMERICA
280-FT LEVEL, WEST, MARBLE

MASSACHUSETTS VOLUNTARY MILITIA, BOSTON
280-FT LEVEL, WEST, GRANITE

FORT GREENE GUARD OF BROOKLYN
140-FT LEVEL, WEST, GRANITE

GEORGIA CONVENTION, 230-FT LEVEL, EAST
ITALIAN MARBLE

GERMAN BENEVOLENT SOCIETY, 40-FT LEVEL, WEST
WHITE MARBLE

HIBERNIAN SOCITY OF BALTIMORE
280-FT LEVEL, WEST, MARBLE

INDEPENDENT ORDER OF UNITED BROTHERS
100-FT LEVEL, WEST, MARBLE

JEFFERSON MEDICAL COLLEGE OF PHILADELPHIA
280-FT LEVEL, WEST, MARBLE

Miscellany
in stone
Stonecutters' art gets
appropriate display on
their stone, which
shows off Doric and
Ionic columns and
other architectural
motifs celebrated in
America's age of Classi-
cal Revival. Actors honor
Shakespeare as well as
Washington; typogra-
phers and photogra-
phers leave their mark.
Military units parade by,
as do German and Irish
immigrants, and citizens
from the hometown of
General Henry Knox,
Washington's first secre-
tary of war. Georgia,
which had sent in a
pro-Union stone in
1851, followed it a year
later with this one,
minus the commentary.

JEFFERSON SOCIETY OF THE UNIVERSITY OF VIRGINIA
270-FT LEVEL, EAST, MARBLE

KINGS COUNTY, NEW YORK
240-FT LEVEL, WEST, BLACK GRANITE

LITTLE FALLS QUARRY, WASHINGTON, D.C.
30-FT LEVEL, EAST, GRANITE

An Exception...

Peter Force, onetime mayor of Washington and an official of the Monument Society, gets in his stone just before a ban on stones from individuals. Sunday school children from New York City quote a proverb— "The Memory of the Just is Blessed." Colleges and a Revolutionary War battleground in Long Island are heard from. Marble offerings come from quarries in Washington, Pennsylvania, and New York. What looks like a blank stone is the faded contribution of mechanics from Raleigh, North Carolina.

MARYLAND PILGRIMS ASSOCIATION OF BALTIMORE
80-FT LEVEL, WEST, MARBLE

MECHANICS OF RALEIGH
90-FT LEVEL, EAST, POSSIBLY GRANITE

METHODIST-EPISCOPAL SUNDAY SCHOOL CHILDREN
NEW YORK CITY, 260-FT LEVEL, WEST, MARBLE

NATIONAL GREYS OF WASHINGTON, D.C.
30-FT LEVEL, EAST, MARBLE

NEW YORK
140-FT LEVEL, WEST, WHITE MARBLE

OAKLAND COLLEGE, MISSISSIPPI
130-FT LEVEL, EAST, WHITE MARBLE

DISTRICT OF COLUMBIA
240-FT LEVEL, WEST, MARBLE

PENNSYLVANIA
140-FT LEVEL, WEST, WHITE MARBLE

PETER FORCE
110-FT LEVEL, EAST, GRANITE

OTTER'S SUMMIT, VIRGINIA
140-FT LEVEL, WEST, GRANITE

THE POSTMASTERS OF INDIANA
110-FT LEVEL, EAST, MARBLE

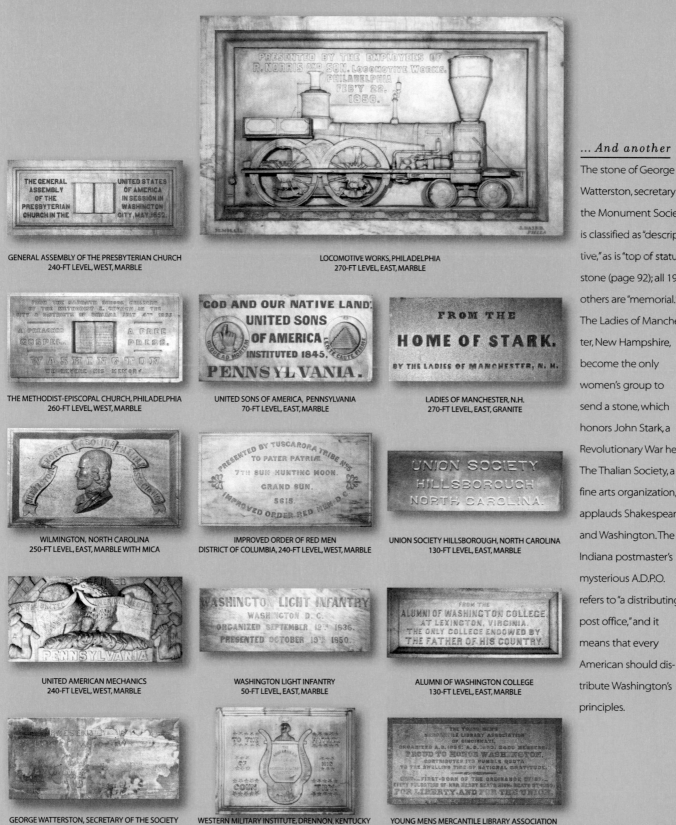

GENERAL ASSEMBLY OF THE PRESBYTERIAN CHURCH
240-FT LEVEL, WEST, MARBLE

LOCOMOTIVE WORKS, PHILADELPHIA
270-FT LEVEL, EAST, MARBLE

THE METHODIST-EPISCOPAL CHURCH, PHILADELPHIA
260-FT LEVEL, WEST, MARBLE

UNITED SONS OF AMERICA, PENNSYLVANIA
70-FT LEVEL, EAST, MARBLE

LADIES OF MANCHESTER, N.H.
270-FT LEVEL, EAST, GRANITE

WILMINGTON, NORTH CAROLINA
250-FT LEVEL, EAST, MARBLE WITH MICA

IMPROVED ORDER OF RED MEN
DISTRICT OF COLUMBIA, 240-FT LEVEL, WEST, MARBLE

UNION SOCIETY HILLSBOROUGH, NORTH CAROLINA
130-FT LEVEL, EAST, MARBLE

UNITED AMERICAN MECHANICS
240-FT LEVEL, WEST, MARBLE

WASHINGTON LIGHT INFANTRY
50-FT LEVEL, EAST, MARBLE

ALUMNI OF WASHINGTON COLLEGE
130-FT LEVEL, EAST, MARBLE

GEORGE WATTERSTON, SECRETARY OF THE SOCIETY
30-FT LEVEL, EAST, SANDSTONE

WESTERN MILITARY INSTITUTE, DRENNON, KENTUCKY
280-FT LEVEL, WEST, MARBLE

YOUNG MENS MERCANTILE LIBRARY ASSOCIATION
OF CINCINNATI, 250-FT LEVEL, EAST, MARBLE

...And another

The stone of George Watterston, secretary of the Monument Society, is classified as "descriptive," as is "top of statue" stone (page 92); all 193 others are "memorial." The Ladies of Manchester, New Hampshire, become the only women's group to send a stone, which honors John Stark, a Revolutionary War hero. The Thalian Society, a fine arts organization, applauds Shakespeare and Washington. The Indiana postmaster's mysterious A.D.P.O. refers to "a distributing post office," and it means that every American should distribute Washington's principles.

Inside the Monument

The Washington Monument, completed in 1885 at a cost of $1.8 million, is the world's tallest freestanding stone structure. For a short time, it was the world's tallest structure until superceded by the Eiffel Tower. Architect Robert Mills' original design evolved into the shape of an Egyptian obelisk in which the height (a) is roughly ten times the width of the base. The final dimensions are 55 feet, 1½ inches at its base, with a height of 555 feet, 5⅛ inches. In 1999, the National Oceanic and Atmospheric Administration, using Global Positioning System technology, pinponted the height at .775 inches taller than the official height. The U.S. Army Corps of Engineers used about 36,000 blocks of marble and granite weighing an estimated 81,000 tons.

a

SKYLINE SENTINELS

The Washington Monument was once the world's tallest building. It was knocked out of first place in 1889 by the Eiffel Tower.

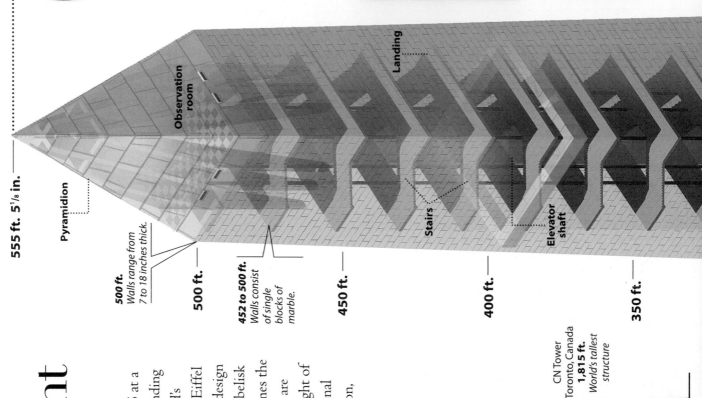

Washington Monument
555 ft.

Eiffel Tower
Paris
984 ft.

CN Tower
Toronto, Canada
1,815 ft.
World's tallest structure

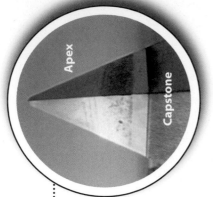

Apex

Capstone

Apex and capstone

The 3,300-pound block of marble atop the monument is the capstone. The apex is a 100-ounce pyramid of solid aluminum—a rare and exotic metal in the 1880s. The East face of the apex is inscribed with the Latin phrase *Laus Deo,* "Praise be to God."

Room with a view

From the observation room at the 500-foot level visitors can see a panorama of the metropolitan Washington area—and far beyond. The West view (above) looks across the Reflecting Pool toward the Lincoln Memorial and into Virginia.

---

555 ft. 5⅛ in.

Pyramidion

Observation room

500 ft.
Walls range from 7 to 18 inches thick.

500 ft.

452 to 500 ft.
Walls consist of single blocks of marble.

Landing

450 ft.

Stairs

Elevator shaft

400 ft.

350 ft.

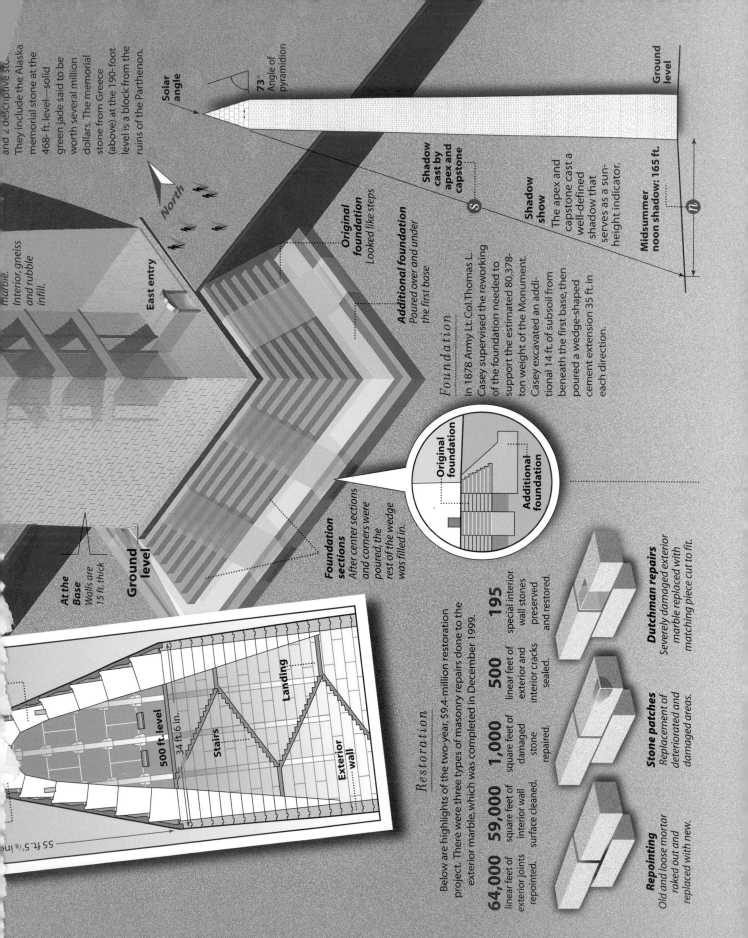

and 2 descriptive sto...
They include the Alaska
memorial stone at the
468-ft. level—solid
green jade said to be
worth several million
dollars. The memorial
stone from Greece
(above) at the 190-foot
level is a block from the
ruins of the Parthenon.

marble.
Interior, gneiss
and rubble
infill.

East entry

North

Solar angle

73°
Angle of pyramidion

Shadow cast by apex and capstone

Shadow show
The apex and
capstone cast a
well-defined
shadow that
serves as a sun-
height indicator.

Midsummer noon shadow: 165 ft.

n

Ground level

Original foundation
Looked like steps

Additional foundation
Poured over and under
the first base

Foundation

In 1878 Army Lt. Col. Thomas L.
Casey supervised the reworking
of the foundation needed to
support the estimated 80,378-
ton weight of the Monument.
Casey excavated an addi-
tional 14 ft. of subsoil from
beneath the first base, then
poured a wedge-shaped
cement extension 35 ft. in
each direction.

Foundation sections
After center sections
and corners were
poured, the
rest of the wedge
was filled in.

Original foundation

Additional foundation

Ground level

At the Base
Walls are
15 ft. thick

55 ft. 5⅛ in.

500 ft. level

34 ft. 6 in.

Landing

Stairs

Exterior wall

Restoration

Below are highlights of the two-year, $9.4-million restoration
project. There were three types of masonry repairs done to the
exterior marble, which was completed in December 1999.

64,000 linear feet of
exterior joints
repointed.

59,000 square feet of
interior wall
surface cleaned.

1,000 square feet of
damaged
stone
repaired.

500 linear feet of
exterior and
interior cracks
sealed.

195 special interior
wall stones
preserved
and restored.

Dutchman repairs
Severely damaged exterior
marble replaced with
matching piece cut to fit.

Stone patches
Replacement of
deteriorated and
damaged areas.

Repointing
Old and loose mortar
raked out and
replaced with new.

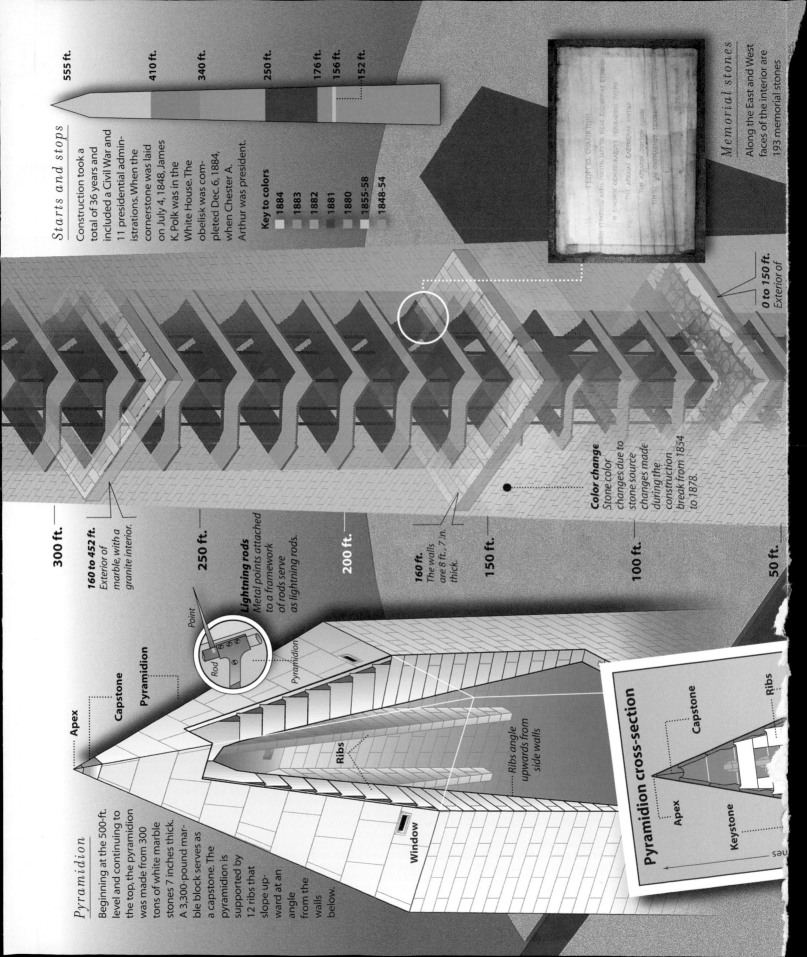

Starts and stops

Construction took a total of 36 years and included a Civil War and 11 presidential administrations. When the cornerstone was laid on July 4, 1848, James K. Polk was in the White House. The obelisk was completed Dec. 6, 1884, when Chester A. Arthur was president.

555 ft.

410 ft.

340 ft.

250 ft.

176 ft.
156 ft.
152 ft.

Key to colors

- 1884
- 1883
- 1882
- 1881
- 1880
- 1855-58
- 1848-54

Memorial stones

Along the East and West faces of the interior are 193 memorial stones

0 to 150 ft.
Exterior of

Color change
Stone color changes due to stone source changes made during the construction break from 1854 to 1878.

160 to 452 ft.
Exterior of marble, with a granite interior.

300 ft.

250 ft.

Lightning rods
Metal points attached to a framework of rods serve as lightning rods.

Point
Rod

200 ft.

160 ft.
The walls are 8 ft. 7 in. thick.

150 ft.

100 ft.

50 ft.

Pyramidion

Beginning at the 500-ft. level and continuing to the top, the pyramidion was made from 300 tons of white marble stones 7 inches thick. A 3,300-pound marble block serves as a capstone. The pyramidion is supported by 12 ribs that slope upward at an angle from the walls below.

Apex
Capstone
Pyramidion

Pyramidion

Ribs

Ribs angle upwards from side walls

Window

Pyramidion cross-section

Apex
Capstone
Keystone
Ribs

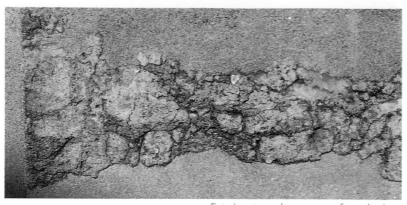

Exterior stone shows scars of weathering.

The millennium restoration

"Washington Monument Dying," said a newspaper headline when the obelisk was hardly twenty years old. The story was based on a geologist's warning that the Monument's stones were rapidly disintegrating. By 1933, when the National Park Service took over the Monument from the U.S. Army Corps of Engineers, chips of the exterior stones were flaking off. In 1992 a structural study commissioned by the Park Service said cracks had appeared, allowing rain to pour in. "It leaks like a sieve," said a Park Service official in 1998. As he spoke, a two-year restoration had begun.

For much of the restoration, the Monument was girded by thirty-seven miles of aluminum scaffolding swathed in translucent blue netting, all designed by architect Michael Graves. "The Eiffel Tower was a temporary structure," Graves says. "My scaffolding is sort of like the Eiffel Tower now." The effect, especially with hundreds of scaffold lights shining at night, was so unexpectedly beautiful that some Washingtonians petitioned to keep the Monument covered.

The $9.4 million restoration, the most extensive ever, was financed through public funds and corporate donors. Experts modernized heating, cooling, and elevator systems; sealed cracks; removed loose mortar from 64,000 linear feet of exterior joints and replaced it with new mortar; cleaned the 59,000 square feet of interior walls; and repaired about 1,000 square feet of exterior stone with marble from the original Maryland quarries.

Restoration specialists (above) chipped away old mortar on the exterior and cleaned every commemorative stone inside the Monument. Clothed for restoration (left), the Monument casts a blue glow at night.

Although the scaffolding touched the Monument, to prevent damage it was not attached.

CHAPTER FIVE

Witness to History

Many Americans who first looked upon the simple, unadorned Monument were disappointed at its plainness. This was the age of American Gothic, of antimacassars on overstuffed parlor chairs, of flowery hats and flowery oratory. It took a foreign visitor to see the mystical power of the Washington Monument. After seeing the Monument in 1890, the English editor of Baedeker's guide to the United States called it "one of the noblest monuments ever raised to mortal man. When gleaming in the westering sun, like a slender, tapering, sky-pointing finger of gold, no finer index can be imagined to direct the gazer to the record of a glorious history." That glorious history would continue in the shadow of the Monument. Its destiny was to be not only a memorial to an American hero but also a magnet for

1963: THE MONUMENT CASTS ITS SHADOW ON THE MARCH ON WASHINGTON.

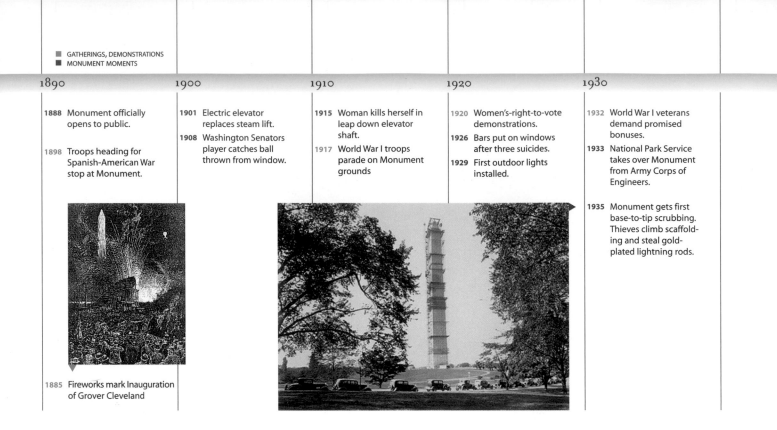

1890   1900   1910   1920   1930

1888 Monument officially opens to public.

1898 Troops heading for Spanish-American War stop at Monument.

1901 Electric elevator replaces steam lift.

1908 Washington Senators player catches ball thrown from window.

1915 Woman kills herself in leap down elevator shaft.

1917 World War I troops parade on Monument grounds

1920 Women's-right-to-vote demonstrations.

1926 Bars put on windows after three suicides.

1929 First outdoor lights installed.

1932 World War I veterans demand promised bonuses.

1933 National Park Service takes over Monument from Army Corps of Engineers.

1935 Monument gets first base-to-tip scrubbing. Thieves climb scaffolding and steal gold-plated lightning rods.

1885 Fireworks mark Inauguration of Grover Cleveland

Americans celebrating life, liberty, and the pursuit of happiness. Fireworks that had etched the sky at the dedication began a tradition that would make the Washington Monument a centerpiece for American happenings, from Shakespeare festivals and rock concerts to revival meetings and kite-flying contests. It also would become the rallying point for gatherings where Americans showed their right to assemble and speak their minds in protest, from the women's suffrage rallies of the 1920s and the Veterans' Bonus March of the 1930s to the anti-war demonstrations of the 1970s. Here too have come those who want their voices to be heard in the distant Congress House.

As the most prominent structure on the Washington landscape, the Monument attracted more than sightseers. In 1908 came Gabby Street, a catcher for the Washington Senators. Gabby bet that he could catch a ball dropped from the top of the Monument. The first of twelve balls slammed against the marble and split open. Gabby caught the thirteenth; the ball was going approximately 125 miles per hour.

Seven years later, a woman plunged down the elevator shaft from the 480-foot landing, becoming the Monument's first suicide. Before 1926, when bars were installed, three men had leaped out of the narrow windows, which are at 504 feet. The bars were later followed by safety glass to prevent people from throwing pennies and splattering fruit. And then, for grimmer reasons, came bulletproof glass.

At first, the Monument was a curiosity—then, as now, the world's tallest freestanding stone structure. To see it, people walked up 893 steps. The trip became easier when the stone-hauling hoist became a passenger elevator in 1887. By the turn of the century, 1,696,718 people had visited the Monument. An electric elevator, installed in 1901, zipped passengers to the top in five minutes.

The completion of the Monument inevitably increased congressional longing for a more monumental Mall. In 1898 Congress began thinking about the centennial of the City of Washington in 1900. President William McKinley convened a committee of the governors of the forty-nine states and territories, who joined with Washington

1945 Biggest crowd ever at war bond rally.
1945 20-millionth visitor.
1946 Truman becomes first president to go to top.
1949 Man leaps down elevator shaft.
1949 Acrobat walks down steps on hands in 1 hour, 25 minutes.
1951 25-millionth visitor.
1954 A marble dropped from window injures woman.
1957 Camera lens drops, breaks woman's hand.
1958 Lighting system turned on to accompany aircraft-warning lights.
1959 Orange thrown from window injures man.

1961 Stilt walker walks up and down steps.
1963 High schoolers piggyback up in 15 miutes, 30 seconds.
1963 Martin Luther King March on Washington.
1964 Man walks up and down the Monument steps in 19½ minutes.
1965 Three men convicted in plot to blow up the Monument, Statue of Liberty, and Liberty Bell.
1968 Poor People's Campaign erects Resurrection City.
1969 Largest anti-war rally draws 250,000.
1969 Farmers demonstrate with tractor invasion.
1964 Monument renovation uses tethered platforms, not scaffolding.

1970 Earth Day marked.
1971 Stairs closed for walking up.
1973 As President Nixon celebrates second Inauguration, 100,000 protest war.
1976 Stairs closed for walking down.
1976 Massive fireworks crowd for U.S. Bicentennial.
1979 150,000 gather for Mass by Pope John Paul II.

1981 Rally for Vietnam War MIAs and POWs.
1982 Man with bomb threatens Monument.
1984 Demonstration against South African apartheid.
1986 National Organization for Women March.
1989 Demonstration against Chinese killing of Tiananmen Square students.

1990 Anti-KKK demonstration.
1994 Bronze statue of Washington placed in lobby.
1995 Million Man March; Park Service stops estimating crowd size.
1998 Most extensive restoration begins.

citizens and Congress to plan a fitting centennial monument on the Mall. No such monument was built. But several plans for the Mall sprouted, including one that would elevate the tracks already there and build a railroad station on the Mall. Railroad executives and members of Congress rolled over that idea with a bill that created one terminal near Capitol Hill for all railroads—palatial Union Station.

Removal of the railroad tracks cleared the way for planners to correct the alignment of the Washington Monument with the Capitol, restoring the symmetry of the Mall that L'Enfant had envisioned. The planners drew a line from the dome of the Capitol to the Monument and declared that this would be the new axis of all future buildings on the Mall. There was more Mall by then, for marshy land along the Potomac had been drained. The draining was particularly hailed by those who believed that the malarial flats had prevented the recovery of wounded President James A. Garfield as he lay dying in 1881.

To balance the Washington Monument on the Mall, some planners saw the possibility of a memorial to Abraham Lincoln. Various grandiose ideas flourished until the creation of the Commission of Fine Arts in 1910. One of the commission's first acts was to recommend that a monument to Lincoln be built on the undeveloped west end of the Mall. A cornerstone was laid in 1915 and the completed Memorial was dedicated on Memorial Day 1922. Lincoln sits in a structure modeled after the Parthenon. So the classical temple that Robert Mills had wanted for George Washington finally was built, but for another president.

By congressional mandate, the Monument will always be the tallest structure in Washington. It looks down upon about half a million people each Fourth of July, upon new Americans saluting its flags each Citizens' Day in September, and upon the faithful Washington National Monument Society on Washington's birthday. On that day, if anyone needs to be reminded, speakers recall once more that this was a man who was "first in war, first in peace, and first in the hearts of his countrymen." He, like his Monument, stands for all that a nation could want.

1892

The Grand Army of the Republic, a Union Army veterans organization, holds its national encampment on the grounds of the Washington Monument, where some had drilled during the Civil War. A highly effective lobbying organization, the GAR established Memorial Day as a national holiday and made veterans an enduring political force. More than 25,000 veterans typically attended a national encampment.

circa 1910

The Washington Monument looms behind President William Howard Taft as he enters the national headquarters of the Daughters of the American Revolution. Founded in 1890, the DAR is open to any woman who can prove direct lineage to an ancestor who served in the Revolutionary War. Taft was the chairman of the commission that oversaw another great monument, the Lincoln Memorial.

1906

Daredevil pilot Lincoln Beachey, dubbed "The Man Who Owns the Sky," flew both aircraft and

dirigibles (opposite). He had once landed on the White House Lawn. Carl Sandburg wrote of him:

> *Only a man,*
>
> > *A far fleck of shadow on the east—*
> >
> > *Sitting at ease*
> >
> > *With his hands on a wheel*
> >
> > *And around him the large gray wings….*

He was killed in 1915 while stunt flying at the Panama Pacific Exposition in San Francisco.

Fireworks explode over the Monument, celebrating the
Inauguration of President Woodrow Wilson to his second term.
In an inaugural address that focused on the threat of war, he said,
"There can be no turning back. Our own fortunes as a nation are
involved whether we would have it so or not." A month later the
United States was at war.

1918

On the ice near the Monument, a graceful skater enjoys a wintry day. He skates on one leg he was born with and one leg that is artificial. A company that manufactured prosthetic devices commissioned the photo. There were 4,403 U.S. amputee casualties during World War I, and their needs inspired revolutionary developments in the creation of artificial limbs.

circa 1920

Rarin' to race, a Hudson Super Six wears its records on its sleek body: 102.5 miles per hour set by Ralph Mulford at Daytona Beach in April, 1916, and 1,819 miles in 24 hours set a few weeks later at a race track in Sheepshead Bay, New York. The first Hudson rolled off the assembly line in Detroit in 1909. The Hudson Super Six, named for its powerful engine, reigned as a racy popular car for decades. A Hudson Super Six made the first two-way, transcontinental trip from New York to San Francisco and back. Cars frequently used the Zero Marker near the Monument as a starting point for cross-country journeys. The marker, dedicated in 1923 by President Warren Harding, is a substitute for a column planned by Pierre L'Enfant "from which all distances" were to measured. It is on the edge of the Ellipse, south of the White House.

1922

National capital as hometown: Swimmers get relief from a muggy summer's day in the tidal basin. Prompted by a disastrous flood in 1881, Congress appropriated money to reclaim the tidal flats along the Potomac, creating more than 600 acres of filled land. The tidal basin, part of the project, was designed to retain water at high tide and release it at low tide. The building of the Jefferson Memorial, dedicated in 1943, changed the shape of the tidal basin, now a tourist attraction, particularly when shoreline cherry trees are in bloom.

1922

On Memorial Day, more than 50,000 people gathered for the dedication of the Lincoln Memorial. The Reflecting Pool between the Lincoln Memorial and Washington Monument was nearly completed. President Warren G. Harding and former President William Howard Taft attended, as did World War I veterans and Robert Todd Lincoln, the only surviving son of the Civil War President. Dr. Robert Moton, president of the Tuskegee Institute, gave the major address but, barred from the whites-only speaker's platform, he had to find a place on the grounds, in the section set aside for black Americans.

1922

Harry Houdini, the most famous escape artist of all time, draws a crowd to watch
him free himself while hanging upside down in a straitjacket suspended from
Keith's Theater, across the street from the Treasury Building. In a 1906 appearance in
Washington, Houdini entered the United States Jail, was stripped naked, searched,
and locked into the cell in which Charles J. Guiteau, the assassin of President
Garfield, was confined. In about two minutes Houdini escaped from the cell, broke
into the cell in which his clothing was locked—and then, to the astonishment of
the witnessing warden, released several prisoners from their cells.

HOUDINI SUSPENDED
IN STRAIGHT JACKET
WASHINGTON JAN 12 1922

1922

The Navy C-7, the world's first lighter-than-air helium airship, circles the Monument.

1933

Like eyes in the night, the red lights of the Monument look down on the Washington waterfront. The lights were installed in 1931 as a warning to aircraft. The waterfront, an open-air market for fishing boats, lies along the Washington Channel, which was changed during the early 1890s when the Army Corps of Engineers filled in tidal flats along the Potomac River. The landfill created a long, narrow island between the river and the mainland. The island, now a park linked by highway to the tidal basin, stretches along the modern waterfront.

1933

President Franklin D. Roosevelt, flanked by his wife Eleanor and his son James, heads for the first of his four Inaugurations. A victim of polio unable to walk unaided, Roosevelt leaned heavily on James's arm as he ascended a special ramp installed on the Senate steps. "The only thing we have to fear is fear itself," he told an America struggling through the Great Depression. This would be the last Inauguration to take place in March. Inaugurations would move to January under the Twentieth Amendment, which was about to be ratified.

1939

More than 75,000 people listen to the voice of Marian Anderson, an internationally famous contralto who had sung before the crowned heads of Europe but was kept out of Washington's Constitution Hall. Its proprietors, the Daughters of the American Revolution, forbade her to appear there because she was black. Outraged, Mrs. Eleanor Roosevelt resigned from the DAR and sponsored Marian Anderson's concert at the Lincoln Memorial. She later became the first African American to perform at New York's Metropolitan Opera.

1945

The last war bond drive of World War II, on July 4, draws the largest crowd yet to assemble at the Monument: 350,000 people. Stars of stage and screen performed at the rally, which came just after victory in Europe and just before victory over Japan. The patriotic throng cheered the greatest Monument fireworks display since the start of the war. At the base of the Monument, Red Skelton, a movie and radio star who went off to the Army, drives a jeep (opposite) loaded with talent, including Marlene Dietrich, Mischa Auer, Lt. William Holden, Dennis O'Keefe, Ethel Merman, and Pvt. John Payne. The rally raised $1,250,000 in bonds, issued by the government to finance the war effort and curb inflation.

1945

A wartime song—"When the lights go on again all over the world"—comes true in Washington as blackout orders end and floodlights bathe the Monument. The first searchlights to shine on the Monument were switched on in 1929. Exterior lighting experiments began in the early 1930s after the installation of red aircraft warning lights in windows on each side of the pyramidion. In 1958-59, to improve visibility, the red flashing lights were put in holes just above the observation windows. New floodlights of more than 92 million candlepower were also set up around the base. The Monument's internal lighting system goes back to 1885, with a system lighting 75 incandescent electric lamps, each rated at 16 candlepower.

Circa 1945

Japan's gift to Washington, cherry trees bloom along the tidal basin. In 1912 First Lady Helen Herron Taft and the Viscountess Chinda, wife of the Japanese Ambassador, planted the first two trees of 3,020. In 1952, cuttings from these trees were returned to Japan to help stabilize trees neglected during World War II. In 1965, Lady Bird Johnson accepted another 3,800 trees, many of which were planted on the grounds of the Washington Monument. Only 125 of the original trees remain.

1947

The Queen of the Cherry Blossoms (opposite) is escorted to her throne by a military aide to President Harry Truman. The annual Cherry Blossom Festival, a District of Columbia rite of spring, challenges the National Park Service's regional horticulturist, who has to predict the date of the blooming well in advance so that the festival can be scheduled. Buds burst into bloom from around mid-March to mid-April.

1948

President Harry Truman leads a three-day Fouth of July celebration of the Monument's centennial. Fireworks, oratory, and a parade marked the anniversary of the Monument's 1848 cornerstone laying. On the *Washington Post*'s float (opposite), comic cutouts, including prizefighter Joe Paloka, join the inevitable bathing beauties that adorned floats of the time. Truman in 1946 became the only president to go to the top of the Monument while in office. He went there to get a view of the proposed site for a bridge across the Potomac River.

circa 1950

Tony Frissell, staff photographer for *Vogue* and *Harper's Bazaar,* uses the Monument as a backdrop for "New Look" fashions. During World War II, she had shifted from fashions to front line, photographing the war at home and overseas. Now, back in fashion, she makes the 19th-century Monument a 20th-century prop. The New Look name came in 1947 when an unknown couturier named Christian Dior launched his new line. After viewing Dior's dresses, Carmel Snow, editor of *Harper's Bazaar,* exclaimed, "Christian, your dresses have such a new look!"

1952

A sightseer looks down upon Washington from the city's highest observation point. Congress has forbidden private construction above 160 feet anywhere in the District of Columbia. The law preserves a low skyline dominated by the Capitol and the Washington Monument.

1957

Kicking up their heels (opposite), spring frolickers—Detroit high schoolers on a field trip—give a newspaper photographer a feature-page standby: a photo with some action in the foreground and the Monument invariably in the background. No one was protesting. It was a time of black-and-white newspaper pages and television screens. People were hula-hooping, digging bomb shelters in the backyard, and listening to Elvis sing about his blue suede shoes.

1965

It's a bird! It's a plane! It's rocketman! Around the Monument at 60 m.p.h.

goes Robert Courter, captain of the Bell Aircraft Rocket Belt Demonstration

Team. The 120-pound rocket belt, developed for the Department of

Defense, could fly for only 20 seconds and was turned down by the

Pentagon. But a stand-in for Sean Connery soared aloft in one of the three

prototypes for a scene in the James Bond movie *Thunderball*.

The Monument becomes the rallying point for Americans drawn to Washington in a crusade for civil rights. The March on Washington took to the nation's capital the beliefs of Martin Luther King, Jr., who had launched his nonviolent campaign for rights in Birmingham, Alabama, in the spring of 1963. After the murder of black leader Medgar Evers in front of his home in Mississippi, President John F. Kennedy met for the first time with civil rights leaders. Kennedy advised against a demonstration in Washington. But civil rights leaders went on planning the march.

1963

"We will not be satisfied until justice rolls down like waters and righteousness like a mighty stream," says the Reverend Martin Luther King, Jr., to a crowd of more than 250,000 Americans of every race and color. "I have a dream my four little children will one day live in a nation where they will not be judged by the color of their skin, but by the content of their character. I have a dream today!" Some 80 million people, among them President Kennedy, saw the rally on television.

1968

The Poor People's Campaign ends with the creation of
Resurrection City, a shantytown that sprawls across the Mall during
one of the most tragic intervals in American history. The Reverend
Martin Luther King, Jr., who had organized the campaign, was
assassinated on April 4, 1968. The Reverend Ralph Abernathy,
successor to King, carried on, sending marchers — black, white,
Indian, and Hispanic — to Washington. They arrived in May and set
up this symbolic community of 2,600 dispossessed citizens. On
June 6 Robert Kennedy died, victim of another assassin. When the
hearse carrying his body passed, the people of Resurrection City
joined in the nation's mourning. On June 24, the city was closed
down by 1,000 police officers using dogs and tear gas.

1969

On Inauguration Day, President-elect Richard M. Nixon meets in the White House with President Lyndon B. Johnson. "After a period of confrontation, we are entering an era of negotiation," Nixon said in his inaugural speech. But the Vietnam War, which had driven Johnson from the White House, would haunt Nixon's presidency. In early 1970 he escalated the war with massive bombing of North Vietnam and attacks on Cambodia.

1970

Anti-war demonstrators clash with supporters of the Vietnam War at a "Win the War Rally" sponsored by a group backing the policies of President Nixon. His expansion of the war into Cambodia had touched off a protest at Kent State University in Ohio, where National Guardsman fired on students, killing four. Anti-war demonstrations surged frequently around the Monument from 1967 to 1973. The largest was on November 15, 1969, when a quarter of a million people, by police estimate, massed at the Monument and peacefully demanded an end to the war.

1971

May Day strips some demonstrators of inhibitions at "Algonquin Peace City," a tent-and-sleeping-bag site full of peace, love, and marijuana. Participants said they wanted to shut down the government. The government responded with arrests of thousands. Such anti-war protests were part of what came to be called the Hippie Movement. Cat Stevens sang what could be their anthem: "If you want to be free, be free, because there's a million things to be."

1974

Veterans join the anti-war movement (opposite). During one demonstration, the National Park Service took down the flags around the Monument, fearing desecration. Infuriated, President Nixon ordered the flags flown day and night. In 1968, Congress passed a law prohibiting the burning or desecration of the flag within the District of Columbia. In 1989 and 1990 the Supreme Court struck down such laws as violations of the free-speech guarantee of the First Amendment.

1991

Men and women who fought in the Persian Gulf War march and fly in a Washington victory parade. Some 800,000 watched the parade, cheering 8,800 troops and combat pilots' flights over the line of march. In the first war with an all-volunteer force since the turn of the century, fighting began with the bombing of Iraq in Operation Desert Shield and ended with the 100 hours of Operation Desert Storm.

1993

Right-to-life supporters (above) leave grim markers behind after a March for Life demonstration. They marched to mark—and condemn—the twentieth anniversary of the Supreme Court's Roe v. Wade decision allowing abortion on demand. At least 75,000 abortion opponents paraded from the Ellipse to Capitol Hill, matching the largest crowd ever at the annual march. Gay rights supporters (opposite) end their day of demonstrations calling for the end of discrimination against lesbians and gay men. They were seeking gay rights laws aimed at government policies that discriminate against homosexuals.

1995

Following the call of Nation of Islam leader Louis Farrakahn, tens of thousands of African-American men come to Washington for the Million Man March. In one of the largest rallies ever seen on the Mall, the men were asked to pledge to "build your own communities, avoid drugs and violence, register to vote, build black political power, and invest in black businesses." Through the years, the National Park Service had been plunged into controversies over crowd estimates on the Mall. The service declined to make an estimate on the Million Man March and said it would not offer crowd counts in the future.

1997

Sweet-tooth patriots celebrate Flag Day (above) with a flag cake measuring

56 by 83 feet and weighing 16,700 pounds. Volunteers assembled it from 1,430

sheet-pan cakes. Tourists got free pieces.

1996

Mourning friends (opposite) search for names on The AIDS Memorial Quilt,

begun in 1985 after more than 1,000 San Franciscans had died from the virus.

The quilt first came to Washington in 1988 with 8,288 panels — each

representing an AIDS victim. By 1999, the quilt had more than 41,000 panels.

Reflections

By a gift of geometry, the tall white shaft of the Washington Monument, which remembers one warrior, appears in the Vietnam Veterans Memorial, which remembers nearly 58,000 warriors. The two black walls of the Vietnam Memorial meet at an angle of 125 degrees, 12 minutes, pointing exactly to the northeast corners of the Washington Monument and Lincoln Memorial. There are fathers here: The Father of His Country and the fathers amid the names. About four of every ten men named on the wall were fathers or were about to become fathers.

Two views from the top

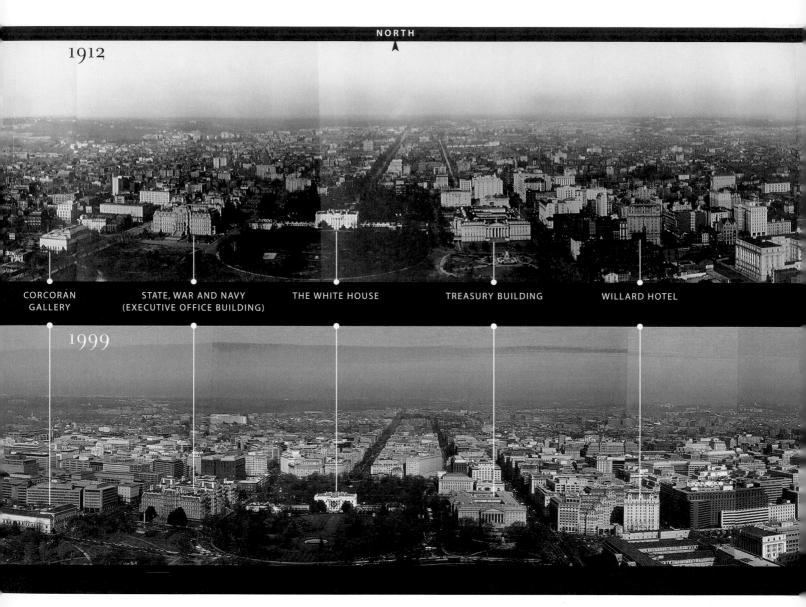

NORTH

1912

CORCORAN
GALLERY

STATE, WAR AND NAVY
(EXECUTIVE OFFICE BUILDING)

THE WHITE HOUSE

TREASURY BUILDING

WILLARD HOTEL

1999

Soon after the Monument was finished, a journalist looked out one of the windows, and saw "a grand view" of the City of Washington, spread "like a toy town, its streets crossing as on a chessboard…." By 1912 the view was still grand, but the city had grown—and so had the federal government. As a guidebook then described the view: "Immediately below, and stretching away to the White House on the north and the Capitol on the east, is the beautiful landscape gardening of the Mall…." In the modern view, the White House and Capitol remain little changed, but the Mall has lost its gardens.

POST OFFICE
BUILDING

MUSEUM OF
NATURAL HISTORY

CAPITOL

SMITHSONIAN
INSTITUTION

REAGAN INTERNATIONAL TRADE CENTER

NATIONAL ARCHIVES

NATIONAL GALLERY

The building that once housed the State, War, and Navy departments now is a branch office of the White House. The old Willard Hotel (guests included President-elect Abraham Lincoln) still stands, though surrounded by new buildings. Red-roofed federal agencies march past the towered Post Office; the newest building is the Reagan International Trade Center. The National Gallery and its East Wing fill a 1912 void along the Mall and the Smithsonian has added (east of the Castle at far right) the round Hirshhorn Museum and the massive National Air and Space Museum.

The Washington Monument, the World's Highest Work of Masonry (555 ft.), from the P. O., Washington, U. S. A.
Copyright 1906, by B. W. Kelley.

ACKNOWLEDGMENTS

The author and editor wish to thank Scottie Allen, Jacinda Davis, Greg della Stua, Jamie Goldblum, Martin Gordon, Sarah Leen, Brian Leonard, W. James Marr, Lynn Medford, Darlene R. Roth, Ph.D., and Maria Sota. Thanks also to the helpful staffs of the Photographs and Prints Division of the Library of Congress, the National Archives, and the Washingtoniana Division of the D.C. Public Library.

Since 1933 the Washington Monument has been part of the United States National Park System. For more information, or to plan a visit, contact the Park Service at:

Superintendent
National Capital Parks, Central
National Park Service
900 Ohio Drive SW
Washington, D.C. 20024

www.nps.gov/wamo/

BIBLIOGRAPHY

The best history of the building of the Washington Monument, with a focus on the work of the U.S. Army Corps of Engineers, is *To the Immortal Name and Memory of George Washington*, written by government historian Louis Torres to mark the centennial of the Monument's completion. (Historic Division, Office of Administrative Services, Office of the Chief of Engineers; published by the Government Printing Office, 1984)

To see Washington evolve from L'Enfant's plan to modern times, turn the well-illustrated pages of *Washington on View: The Nation's Capital Since 1790* by John W. Reps. (University of North Carolina Press, 1991). Information on the man most responsible for finishing the Monument came from *Memoir of Thomas Lincoln Casey (1831-1896)* by Henry L. Abbot (National Academy of Sciences, 1897).

Other publications of interest: *Guide and Index to the Papers of Robert Mills, 1781-1855* edited by Pamela Scott (Scholarly Resources, 1990); *Dedication of the Washington National Monument February 21, 1885* (reading copy provided courtesy of the National Park Service); *History of the Washington National Monument and Washington National Monument Society,* compiled by Frederick L. Harvey, secretary of the society (Government Printing Office, 1903).

The biographical information on George Washington came from many sources, particularly *Writings of George Washington,* edited by John C. Fitzpatrick and obtained through the "George Washington Papers" web sites of the Library of Congress and the University of Virginia. "Father Figure," the George Washington chapter in Robert Shogan's *The Double-Edged Sword* (Westview, 1999), was valuable as a source that linked Washington's character to modern politics.

Other sources: *All Cloudless Glory,* Vol. II, *Making a Nation,* by Harrison Clark (Regnery, 1996); *Ask Mr. Foster Guide to Washington* (Standard Guide Information Office, 1911); *The Americans,* Vol. II, The National Experience, by Daniel J. Boorstin (Vintage Books, 1965); *The Dye Is Now Cast* by Lillian B. Miller (Smithsonian Institution Press, 1975); *The First Federal Congress 1789-1791* by Margaret C. S. Christman (Smithsonian Institution Press, 1989); *Founding Father: Rediscovering George Washington* by Richard Brookhiser (Free Press, 1996); *The Genius of George Washington* by Edmund S. Morgan (Norton, 1980); *George Washington an American Icon* by Wendy Wick (National Portrait Gallery/Barra Foundation, 1982); *George Washington Man and Monument* by Frank Freidel and Lonnelle Aikman (National Geographic Society, 1973); *George Washington's Mount Vernon* by Benson J. Lossing (Fairfax Press); *On This Spot, Pinpointing the Past in Washington, D.C.,* by Douglas E. Evelyn and Paul Dickson (National Geographic Society, 1999); *Picturesque Washington* by Joseph West Moore (J.A. & R.A. Reid, 1888); *Patriarch: George Washington and the New American Nation* by Richard Norton Smith (Houghton Mifflin, 1993); *Washington,* an abridgment by Richard Harwell of the seven-volume *George Washington* by Douglas Southall Freeman (Scribner's, 1968).